AF251570

WINDYMARE
120 ACRES

POTPOURRI FROM KETTLE LAND

Area of highest hill in Manitowoc County - Elevation 1047 feet

Hard woods
Brush
Raspberry Patch
Orchard
Hill Driveway
Barn
House
Sheds
Fire Lane
Hill Lane
2 Hill Lane

Scattered Brush
Hollow with Rocks
wild apple tree
Aspen Trees
Hollow with Rocks
Spruce trees
Grass Knoll
Hollow Rock Filled
Wide Firelane
Pine Tree Plantation
Narrow Fire Lane
Pine Tree Plantation
Fire Lane

Rim Ridge Lane
Wild Grape and Wild Plum
Sumac
Deep Hollow
Knoll with wild apple tree
Deer Trail
East Ridge Trail
Hollow
Second East Ridge
Hill Meadows
wild asparagus
Deer Trails
morels
Aspen Trees

Kettle Lake
Hardwood Trees and Pines
Bog Low wet land
TOWN ROAD
steep Hill - Hardwoods
Pines and Hardwoods
Swamp
Small Hills

Swampy area
Cedar Trees
Fire Lane
Grassy Knoll
Scattered Brush

Scattered Hardwood and Pine Trees (white)
Deep Hollow
Grass Knoll
Grass Knoll

Steep Rising Forested Hill
Hardwood and White Pine Trees
Aspen Trees
Wild Apple Tree
Steep Rising Forested Hill

N
E
S
W

Private Property
County Park

ISBN 1-886028-46-X

Library of Congress Catalog Card Number: 00-102845

Published by:

Savage Press
P.O. Box 115
Superior, WI 54880

715-394-9513

e-mail: savpress@spacestar.com

Visit us at: www.savpress.com

Printed in the USA.

POTPOURRI *from* KETTLE LAND

120 Wooded Glacial Hill Acres
Become A Mentor For Country Living

by Irene I. Luethge

Illustrated
by Irene I. Luethge

Savage PRESS

Box 115, Superior, WI 54880 (715) 394-9513

To my mother, father and doctor grandfather who introduced me to this enchanting place in my youth and to the many friends who urged me to write about what happened after I went to live on the land.

MY MENTOR,
THE LAND

s I moved toward and into retirement years and recorded my adventures in annual Christmas letters I found myself realizing I had discovered the pot at the end of the rainbow - it was on my 120 wild Kettle Moraine acre land. No longer did I feel an attraction to experiences and interests that existed elsewhere. The world that captured my attention was condensed right there and the land reached out to me with an array of offerings and sense of peace.

The land became my teacher. It shared its wisdom about wild and growing things. It tested my coping skills through its seasons. It gave me souvenirs from its history. It made me into a conservationist, wary of man's destructive powers and interference.

The land nourished me. It fed my eyes with scenic beauty; it fed my senses with fragrances and sounds; and it fed my palate with samplings from its pantry. It stimulated pursuits of my hobbies – painting, photography, woodcarving, vegetable dying, and designing rugs to hook.

The land assumed the role of physician's helper. It soothed me in times of crises and gave me the will and purpose to carry on. I came through a succession of health problems and in 1979 a diagnosis, referred to by some people as a "death sentence" was made. I have survived beyond the future predicted, living on borrowed time some call it. My appreciation of the world around me intensified.

My senses of sight, smell and touch became more acute as I walked the land. I was no longer pushing myself into the future but rather savoring even the minute details of each day as fully as I could.

The land was named Windymare – named when my doctor grandfather and I vacationed in my youth on the land's pioneer farmstead. The land began a claim on my heart that lasted over subsequent years and eventually brought me back as its owner.

So much encouragement from recipients of my annual Christmas letters precipitated writing with more details this collection of the experiences Windymare's land gave me from the 1930's and on to October 27, 1944.

Irene I. Luethge

TABLE OF CONTENTS

TABLE OF CONTENTS

THE LAND
BECKONS

Chapter I

THE LAY OF THE LAND

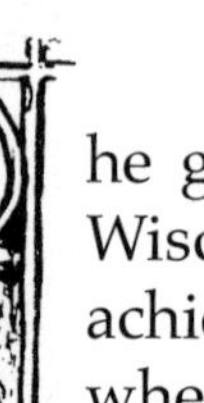

he glacially sculptured landscape in eastern Wisconsin, known as the Kettle Moraine, achieved national attention in October 1970 when Richard Nixon, then President of the United States, put his signature on a bill creating the Ice Age National Park on lands within the area.

The deep-sided pits indenting this land were called "kettles" by ancestors who likened them to cooking pots. The French word "moraine" originated with Alpine peasants to describe the soil and rock laid down by glaciers to form ridges over the land. This unique land formation stretches far beyond the irregular elongated boundaries of the Park. I live on the northern end of an interlobate stretching between Manitowoc County and Whitewater in southeastern Wisconsin.

Twenty thousand years or so ago two lobes of a great ice sheet met with such tremendous force that the ice heaved, cracked, buckled and melted. Boulders, sand and gravel were caught in the pile-ups and numerous small lakes (like one on my property) formed. Some eventually succumbed to man's alterations.

Receding glaciers designed the eastern side of Wisconsin, a mitten shaped state. Its thumb, the scenic Door County peninsula shares the same Lake Michigan shoreline that extends southward past Manitowoc, Sheboygan (where I was born), to Milwaukee and down to

Chicago. An hour's drive southward from the inner base of the thumb at Green Bay lies Kiel (my postal address).

Kiel, population about 3,100, is the small business hub of a farming area that has worn away many features of the glacial land. Kiel, settled by Germans in 1852, was surrounded by Indian encampments, some on my property where hunting was good and adjacent Cedar Lake offered abundant fishing. On the east end of Kiel's present short main street of updated old-time buildings stands an 1852 fieldstone grain mill beside the mill pond. The Sheboygan River spills over its dam en route eastward after paralleling the main street and originating in the Sheboygan Marsh to the west. Kiel's eastern outskirts face a series of nearby hills whose highest point I claim as home.

Between Kiel and my 120 acres of hilly wooded land, the Sheboygan River part way follows a curvy meandering road that eventually passes my land, forking at Cedar Lake. Before this road underwent remodeling it erupted near my land with sinkholes during snowmelts and rainy spells. What was a gravel road has since been black topped, numbered mailboxes identify increased property owners and it lost its RFD (Rural Free Delivery) designation in favor of a name. Desired access to this secluded out-of-the-way area brought on the break-up of relatively virgin wooded acreage into several salable real estate parcels.

The sink holes that plagued the old road marked a former stream bed whose water wound its way to the Sheboygan River, originating from spring snow melts on the hills, overflow from my lake and springs that dotted the area. My land at that end still retains some standing water year-round and nourishes a magnificent stand of ferns. Long ago before man rearranged the glacier's landscaping, my lake and Cedar Lake just beyond were connected.

The road makes a curve, trees arc the road and my driveway veers off sharply up a steep hill. Opposite at the road's edge a precipitous drop ends in the boggy shoreline along my half of the Kettle lake. Across the tree rimmed eight or so acre lake, rolling cultivated and grazing fields rise from the shoreline. An aged farmhouse, red barn and gleaming new silos stand in a grove of trees at one side, the only signs of a near neighbor visible from my hilltop.

The lake and its bordering bog and trees attract waterfowl, and the migratory birds that make rest stops from their overhead fly-routes. Whistling swans rest a day or two en route to their Green Bay stop. Muskrats populate the lake's marshy parts and wood ducks raise families in the many hollow trees beside the boggy mats. Both Great Blue Herons and Green Herons hover around the water's edge. Most colorful and vocal, the Red Winged and Yellow Headed Blackbirds bring song to the lake in early spring as they sit on swaying cattails. The Red Winged male arrives from the south before the last of spring's wintry storms, stakes out his territory, preens and puffs out his bright red and yellow shoulder coverts before the females arrive and calls "Look at ME! Look at ME!"

Spring officially is announced by the build-up of the spring peepers chorus as soon as the lake ice melts into blue water. These tiny frogs, the size of a thumbnail, inflate a little bubble in their throats, which results in something between a chirp and a whistle. The sound I hear on my hilltop resembles tiny sleigh bells saying "pinkletink" but not in unison. Nature books call them Pickering Hyla whose chameleon-like color changes from light grayish or yellowish-brown to darker shades. Some old timers have called them "Pinkletinks". By late spring their voices have achieved enough volume to drown out competing sounds except for the throaty deep-voiced bullfrogs.

Beyond my driveway going eastward along the winding, densely wooded Town Road, about a quarter mile, the road forks where it meets the swampy edge of Cedar Lake. A left turn plus a half mile north brings one to Louis Corners – a tavern, a house, a woodlot and a plain white steepled church set on a knoll beside a graveyard. I see this cluster from my hilltop and on Sunday mornings hear the organ and singing congregation if windows are open and a wind blows southward.

A right turn going south at the fork leads to Highway #32 via a roller-coaster ride of steep hills and far reaching vistas. In fall the hilly-forested background becomes a colorama spectacle. It is this route that connects with the highway to Sheboygan; first traveled in my youth when Jenny, an overloaded 1917 Dodge transported enough furnishings and supplies to convert an old farmstead to a habitable vacation spot that eventually became Windymare.

"And how much land do you have?" I'm often asked.

"On the level it's 120 acres of hills but it also reaches to the center of the earth in one direction and in the other takes in the stars," I answer.

CHAPTER FOOTNOTES
*Gores, Henry, **Yellowbird, A True Tale of The Early Settlement of Town Schleswig, Manitowoc County** (Northwestern Steam Print, Manitowoc, WI 1900)*

***Manitowoc County Outdoors** (Conservation Education Inc. of Manitowoc County and Manitowoc County Soil and Water Conservation District, Manitowoc WI 54220 1967)*

Chapter II

JENNY

hen grandfather bought Jenny he reluctantly gave in to the auto age with visions of her glamorous companionship but dubious about her endurance and longevity. Anybody who was somebody owned an auto and everybody else tried to have one, especially the more affordable flivers or Tin Lizzies as the first Fords were called. Only the iceman and the milkman appeared unaffected. Their surefooted horses plus a jingle of harnesses and slow clop-clop of hooves gave a more comforting sound on Sheboygan's streets than the noisy erratic autos.

Jenny, a 1917 Dodge Roadster, replaced my doctor grandfather's horse and buggy in the barn next door. I was too little to know what the furor was about except that his buggy and horse equipment got moved no further than the barn's second floor. Their future depended on Jenny's comparative efficiency in handling grandfather's house calls.

Just as grandfather customarily picked his horses for disposition and conformation, he chose Jenny for her style and classiness despite reservations about her dependability. She was elegant: modest in shiny black; isinglass windows on the sides and rear of the leather-like hood covering the single front bench-seat; black iron ears protruded on each side as grab bars to aid stepping onto the high runningboard; a slanted rear trunk that resembled a bustle;

and four tall slender wheels that looked too frail to cope with thick mud on country roads.

Occasionally when he made house calls I was hoisted up to the front seat beside grandfather. Sometimes he carried on conversations with Jenny instead of me. I never understood them.

When she wasn't fully under control he hollered "Whoa! Whoa!" till she slowed down or came to a stop. If she chose not to, he showed her the horsewhip lying on the car seat and shouted German words unfamiliar to my ears. A balky motor lacked the control and warm empathy he was accustomed to between his horse and himself.

Chauffeuring grandfather during the ensuing years in all kinds of weather on day and night calls took a toll on Jenny's jaunty appearance but won grandfather's respect. He decided on a different assignment for Jenny when the four-door new Buick took over. He thought she could haul rocks, shrubs and plants to his city garden from the pioneer farm property he purchased – 120 acres of wild wooded Kettle Moraine hills 27 miles northwest of Sheboygan. Jenny's bustle-like rear trunk could be reconstructed as a truck platform. In turn, she could haul necessities to the old log house on the property, making it habitable for vacations and extended overnights. Jenny would be indispensable.

For her new assignment she would be stripped down to bare essentials. The once proud, handsome eye-catching damsel was destined to become a hard working laborer and housed in a dusty age-old hand-hewn barn inhabited by sparrows, pigeons, squirrels and mice. Her work would include hauling firewood from the woods, rocks for building projects, manure from nearby farms for fertilizing, gravel for driveway repairs and other demeaning jobs.

Her fate was sealed the day our big move took place, action that replaced talk. None of us sensed the impact this day would have on our futures. By late morning Jenny was barely visible under a load of cast-off furniture, kitchen equipment, boxes and tools piled high. My teenage frame sat crammed between grandfather at the wheel and Vic, our collie. Jenny had to be cranked up front, buttons pulled on the dashboard, then a jerk and we jounced off down the road. Behind us followed an equally overloaded 4-door Ford touring car where my parents merged into the stacks of boxes inside, balanced by more boxes strapped to the running boards.

Our entourage, akin to a gypsy caravan, was noisy. With grandfather in the lead tooting Jenny's horn that sounded like a herd of bellowing elephants, any interference at crossroads was kept at bay. Vic's shrill voice barked his opinions, howling when Jenny bellowed. Father, behind us, tooted his horn as assurance he was there.

This went on for 27 miles, half over hilly dusty dirt roads, before we reached the steep hill driveway up to the farm. Jenny's tall slim wheels never faltered under the load as she climbed. She gasped noisily and sounded asthmatic but time proved this to be her characteristic on hills, her perseverance was admirable. Father's sturdier looking car, on the other hand, balked and steamed and gave up before reaching the hilltop.

That steep wooded hill driveway under a canopy of interlocking tree branches led to Jenny's new home and a breathtaking panoramic view from the hilltop. It seemed to me that we looked down over the world from heaven. This bit of heaven consisted of a log house nearly overgrown with flowering vines, a singing windmill, a silvery timbered barn, fruit trees and wild flowers in bloom. A mix of fragrances spread a mist of enchantment. I absorbed it. It soaked in enough to draw me back longingly as years took me further away.

Through the following years Jenny's rugged constitution never needed attention from a mechanic, my father's loving tinkering took care of any passing ailments. Somehow the magnetism of this place must have stroked us all with its restorative powers: it kept Jenny's health in prime condition; it influenced my folks to replace the log house with a permanent one so they could relocate here after grandfather died; it attracted Blackie, a stray black Lab, to adopt the whole 120 acres when Vic, our collie, departed for Doggie Heaven and gave Jenny another front seat helper.

That magnetism of the enchanted hilltop even succeeded in deciding my return too after years of living in other parts of the country. Taking over ownership included a working partnership with Jenny. Our most ambitious time consuming project was the hauling of fieldstones to build a fireplace that would span much of the family room west wall.

To get to the fieldstones located in the far back acres where they had been tossed into two Kettle hollows, tired old Jenny navigated countless trips uncomplainingly, bouncing over the rough terrain of the hilly south firelane. Pioneer farmers must have worn themselves out trying to clear the land of stones which they dumped in the hollows before realizing that the glaciers centuries ago meant the rocks to be the land's chief crop.

Whether Jenny's groans resulted from the strain of feeling the thundering roll of rocks I tossed into her rear end carrier or voiced impatience over my communion with ancient history, I couldn't tell. Sorting out colorful rocks and discovering imbedded fossils slowed me down as my mind's eye saw glaciers bulldozing this place which at one time may have been washed by tropical seas. The spin-off came evenings when I searched books for identification of my findings. Inadvertently I gave myself a geology course. Jenny benefited from that. She stood passively as I lectured on my newfound knowledge. These souvenirs from thousands of years ago that she was transporting would be displayed in a new age fireplace wall that would do honor to her efforts.

Heavily weighed down, Jenny's delicate appearing wheels ground into the dirt to get started and again on the steep hillsides. She heaved, squealed and sneezed but never faltered, leaving an ever-deepening trail of ruts behind as proof of her effort. With Blackie nipping at her tires between leaps onto the front seat to bark orders, she was spurred on.

The west wall fireplace finally became a finished reality. It glistened in sunshine or moonlight, and like a chameleon made color changes in rainy weather. It became the showpiece of the house. I like to think of it as a memorial to Jenny's labors.

One day some weeks later a young couple arrived on my hilltop to introduce themselves as old-time car collectors. They had seen Jenny in Kiel and traced her to this address. They wanted to buy her though appearances were no longer flattering. She could be restored to the once eye-catching stylish figure of earlier days, they said. We found her dismantled parts stored in the barn loft and dusted them off.

How could I deprive Jenny of this Cinderella opportunity and its reward for years of hard work? She was wanted and would be appreciated. I brushed a few tears from my eyes as she was driven away.

Occasionally at showings of old cars or glimpses of them on television I'm able to spot Jenny. She is a Grand Old Lady now, flaunting no scars from her hard working years on my land.

Chapter III

A PLACE NAMED WINDYMARE

"We ought to call these 120 acres something other than 'The Farm.' Nobody ever lived on the land long enough to attach a name. Got any ideas?" asked my doctor grandfather.

I had turned teenager a month ago in August and we'd been spending weekends making the place habitable for vacationing. At the time I was infatuated with horses and riding so a horsey name was uppermost in my mind. In fact, I fantasized a horse or two occupying the empty barn stalls and cantering over these Kettle Moraine hills.

My folks believed in the practical and would have settled on a name like The Farm, Deer Trails, Timber Hills or something equally unimaginative. My father went so far as to suggest Bean Soup to honor mother's specialty and excellent cooking.

For a while we argued about "when is a farm not a farm?" A small vegetable patch, the beginnings of rock gardens with flowers, a weathered barn containing empty stalls, a chickenless chicken coop turned workshop, a windmill to pump water, a privy with a view, a vine covered log house, and a shed to store firewood and Jenny (the 1917 Dodge laborer), and a couple orchard trees didn't add up to the dictionary's definition of a place devoted to agriculture and produce.

Then we talked about the land's reputation for Indian encampments and hunting grounds where Indian artifacts showed up on our hikes. We searched out Indian names and words but reached no agreement on suitability. Our fossil findings and the glacial history of the land produced no name ideas either.

My doctor grandfather, a water-color painter and landscape gardener by hobby, said he dreamed of building a rustic shack on the hilltop's high-est ground for a studio and a place to spy on the coming and goings of animal life. He wanted to hear the wind whistle around the tim-bers, feel its coolness on hot days and watch the wind ruf-fle trees and grasses. He thought maybe the animals or the wind could help us figure out a name.

My strongest bond to grandfather at this time was our mutual love of horses. We talked about the horses who piloted and looked after him in his horse and buggy days and I told him about my favorites at the riding stable in Sheboygan. I wondered if we could work something horsey into the name of this place.

The day we decided on a name grandfather and I had hiked deer trails all afternoon, nibbling our usual snack of ginger snaps and apples stuffed into our knicker pockets. The knickers we wore had deep pockets, fit loose and fastened in a tight band below the knee. Knee-high laced leather boots and our most frayed old sweaters, more burr resistant, completed our Alpine climber look. We usually ended our hikes on the highest ground of the hilltop so we could cool off in the breezes and feast our eyes on the view. We looked down past the few orchard trees to the log house about 100 feet beyond, then down the hill's wooded slope to the lake and the broad expanse of rolling hills, pastures and woodlands beyond.

Grandfather could be counted on to remark, "Coolest, most beautiful spot in the whole world on a hot day!" When the winds kicked up making trees fling about it looked to our horse smitten eyes like herds of horses tossing their manes as they galloped over the hills. Grandfather pointed this out to me one time and I said the breezes even combed the land's hair when they passed through the grasses.

"Got a name picked out yet?" Grandfather asked me.

"How about WINDY MARE?" I asked.

"Agreed", grandfather said, and we sifted some grains of earth through our fingers for the wind to carry off in a baptismal gesture.

THE BARNYARD SKYSCRAPER

y first glimpse of a real live windmill occurred the day overloaded Jenny, the 1917 Dodge, sneezed and wheezed her way up the steep hill driveway for the first time. The windmill towered over an enchanting vine covered log house that stood beside it, dwarfing the age worn pioneer farmstead and even the backdrop of woodlands and hills. The silvered iron framework, reaching up into the heavens, was a fifty foot mechanical marvel that purred and squealed happily to the accompaniment of the pump's clink-clink as it hauled water up and out of the earth's depths. I fell under its spell.

That spell was a feel for country life. Bees humming, birds chattering, distant cows mooing and dogs yapping made an accompaniment that sounded like a dance band in warm-up practice with the windmill's rhythms. Add to this the air's incense of blossoms and grasses on a bright sunny day.

My youthful enthusiasm welcomed the adventure of converting a pioneer farmstead into a make-do habitable place to spend weekends and vacations. Before I even touched ground my teenage imagination was exploring the wooded hills, investigating the Kettle lake below the hilltop and cavorting with the windmill, all just twenty-seven miles northwest of my Sheboygan home and purchased by my doctor grandfather. We – my mother, father and grandfather – were among a newly emerging breed of town folks acting on a yen for "the simpler life" instead of the north woods resort retreats we knew.

It was no fluke that a working windmill should captivate me because I had lived my whole young life with silent varieties painted on my bedroom furniture and embroidered on sheets and pillow cases. They were Dutch style, different from this real one and I had to find out why. Little did I surmise what curiosity would produce.

I found out that Dutch windmills showed up in North America as early as 1622 at the Virginia Colony but the style proved too heavy, complex and expensive for the simple task of pumping water. In 1854, Dan Halladay, a Connecticut machine shop owner, patented a simple wooden windmill skeleton. It improved on European designs, a special governor weight kept the wheel from running away in a gale. Antique collectors want these. Another inventor, Rev. Leonard Wheeler, a missionary to Wisconsin Indians, developed a folding vane and sail for windmills that made them face into the wind when in use and lock parallel to the wind when not.

The handles evidently worked like the wooden grip attached to one of my windmill's legs that I was allowed to pull, making the wheel turn on or off when released. Finding out that I could start or stop the silver wheel spinning against the blue sky made me join its happy squeals when tail shifts caught wind changes. Grandfather said that harnessing wind energy like this to produce power dated back to earliest times in history. Sailing ships had depended on it. Farmers needed it to get water out of the ground too and for grinding grains into food. For centuries the mechanical slaves kept cattle and families alive, watered plantings that put food on the table and subsequently money in pockets as produce was sold. The windmill was the hub of the farmyard, synonymous with survival.

The hub of our weedy farmyard no longer watered cattle, chickens and crops, servicing instead our washing, cooking, refrigeration and thirst needs. The absence of water piped into the log house required manpower to keep two white enamel pails, sitting on a kitchen bench, filled with water. A dipper substituted for a spigot to mete out the water. Bathing was done either as a sponge bath in a shallow enamel basin or by a shower.

Showering was least electrifying when done in late afternoon after the sun had warmed the icy water in the two-person water tank. The tank, mounted on a tall iron stand beside the pump house, was hose connected at its top to receive pumped water that it discharged through a spray spigot on its bottom. Four corner posts held up privacy canvas sheets that on windy days gave exposure peeks.

Our refrigerator was a big galvanized wash tub sitting under the pump's spout in the pumphouse and filled with icy water. Milk jars and food containers were weighted down with rocks on their lids to withstand the forceful gush of water when the pump was in operation. Occasionally the force toppled a can whose contents joined the tub's overflow and merrily sailed down the outside run-off trough, past the privy and down the hillside.

The privy, among lilac bushes at the hill's brink was minus plumbing, but dallying users often were mesmerized by the windmill's singing plus the view. The two seater offered one of the best sights, door left ajar, of Cedar Lake's blue waters a half-mile distant. Visits from curious wildlife creatures in search of escaped foods sailing the run-off trough became common place for us but disconcerting for visitors.

Our senses seemed always attuned to the windmill's presence. If sounds changed we reacted with alarm. Windmills in general held a reputation for easy and minimal maintenance and every farmer knew what to do if they balked. Father wasn't a farmer so when the blades on our mechanical marvel slowed, grinding as if in agonizing pain, he sought farmer advice. He was told to climb up the narrow rung ladder on the leg of the mill, carrying a long spouted oilcan in one hand. Upon mounting the tiny wooden platform high up, the trick was to hang on with one hand and stretch with the other to pour grease into the gear box. Like watching a high wire trapeze performer we froze with anxiety as father balanced precariously until the blades were nourished and resumed their rhythmic music.

My opportunity to find out more about these fascinating structures occurred at the County Fair lay-out of farm machinery. Ours was a standard steel skeleton, probably one of the models designed by LaVerne Noyes, the founder of the Aeromoter Company. When first produced it was considered a joke but ended in cornering the million dollars sales market. Windmills became almost as important as railroads for opening up prairie states and the dry southwest to agriculture. They were the boss of the farm, cost $50.00 and were expected to last fifty years – so owners seldom could grumble about a mechanical slave that required little oil and few repairs.

Our barnyard boss undoubtedly had labored for more than fifty years so it was no wonder that its sturdiness and rust spots succumbed to the abuse of wind and winter storms. One night we were wakened by deafening bangings as if machine gun shots were bombarding the house. Fearful for our lives, courage to investigate came slowly. A rusted blade was banging loose on the wildly moving mill's wheel.

Recognizing that the mill was aging, father decided to install a Kohler generator to do the pumping and more, retiring much of the mill's operation. He was influenced too by unsuccessful tinkering, trying to harness the wind's energy with the mill's efforts enabling storage in a battery that would bring light to a kitchen bulb on a wire strung between kitchen and pumphouse. Only a few flickers resulted. Kerosene lamps prevailed.

The day that electricity came up the hill and a forty foot post carrying green glass transformers was set in the ground, this pioneer farmstead and our "simpler life" ideas were targeted for change. Grandfather died. My folks replaced the termite damaged log house with a permanent year-round home and the windmill's skeleton was disconnected from the well and moved thirty feet to the edge of the driveway's barnyard turn-around. Eventually I took over ownership.

For a brief time the mill's frame, minus wheel and blades, was topped by a tenement barrel-dwelling for purple martins who filled the air with lively chortles and ballet flying maneuvers. Weather demolished the barrel and the iron skeleton lost its last musical contribution. An arm, extending horizontally, was welded onto the top to hold a mercury light. When lit only a faint hum resulted.

Today's power lines and poles etch new silhouettes across the landscape where once the skyscrapers of the barnyard presided. I'm glad my windmill frame survives and keeps alive its heritage of giving service. Wild grape, bittersweet and honeysuckle vines have twined their way up the mill's legs, anchoring again the silvered framework to the land.

Chapter V

THE PARLOR STOVE

n the time Riverside Aer, Duct. No 14, patented 1911, was removed from two Sheboygan houses and a barn, then taken twenty seven miles to the wee parlor of Windymare's ancient log house, our vacation retreat, twenty years elapsed. The Aer had acquired the respect and ominous dignity of a Burnhilde and the temperament of a Carmen. An opera star she wasn't but she knew how to take center stage. Yet she was a warm-hearted ruler of the household with potential for a promising mellowed and adaptable old age.

Ensconced in the log house parlor her bulk scarcely left enough room for the cot, on which my teenage body slept on vacation nights, and the four chairs that family or guests occupied for conversation. The Aer not only over-warmed that room but had to extend her influence to the two tiny bedrooms on the parlor's side and into the adjacent kitchen. Originally it was thought to put her in the kitchen on the black stained part of the wide pine floor boards where an iron range must have stood for years. But the Aer was a parlor stove incapable of cooking meals. Instead a three-burner blue metal kerosene stove had to cook our meals but couldn't heat the kitchen where we liked to sit around the center table under the hanging kerosene lamp.

At 5 $^1/_2$ feet tall the Aer sported enough shiny nickel trim to catch many an admiring eye. She wore an urn-like nickel top-piece on a small cut-work collar that swung aside so an iron grill plate could keep a coffee pot or cook pot hot or hold the granite bowl in which my mother put bread dough to rise. Below that lay an embossed iron shoulder edged with a flaring nickel collar. Underneath was a curved iron door with three isinglass windows through which I liked to watch the fire flicker inside. The glossy pearly luster of the windows bespoke of their earthly origin in mica that formed in igneous and metamorphic rock. Dramatically flaring below the door was a nickel skirt decorated with cutwork that we adapted as holders for wet mittens and socks in need of drying. The skirt was too slippery to serve as a foot rest unless we reclined in chairs so stocking footed toes could hook into the openings to hold a foot in place. Under the skirt and above the bulging nickel bottom with its curved feet was the ash box, which had to be emptied daily even though it blew dust in our faces.

The whole hulk stood on a five foot square metal mat painted to look like an oriental carpet out of the ARABIAN NIGHTS TALES, the kind that sailed off to exotic places. It was often a conversation piece as we sipped steaming hot chocolate to warm bodies frozen outdoors. The kettle of hot chocolate sitting on the stove's top iron grill spread an enticing aroma, soon sullied by the smell of wet wool hung beside the Aer to dry. If we opened the iron door to toast marshmallows over the coals, as we sometimes did in the evening, the oriental mat caught the droppings.

The Aer was our first thought both at day's start and at day's end. Mornings the near dead embers needed a vigorous shaking down before kindling and coals could be added. I tried to help by blowing up the flames till I reeled from dizziness. Father usually took over by shoveling more coals on the firebed plus a dollop of kerosene. Boom! And a roar of flames tore up the chimney. Evenings were undramatic but noisy as he shook the coal bucket till all embers were heavily covered. The fire was banked for the night.

A banked coal bed maintained fiery embers all night without refueling if the small slits on the sides of the stove's belly, regulated by cogged wheels, were set so only minimal air entered. When coordinated with the stove pipe key, that regulated a disk, it controlled air drawn into the stove's chimney. Herein lay Aer's temperamental nerve. Without warning she could puff clouds of smoke through the slits and crevices, quickly filling the room. It was the Aer's most effective attention getting device.

Her other device was the downdraft that developed in the chimney. She sounded a loud piff and the whole Aer became engulfed in a cloud of smoke as if a wizard had worked his magic. Getting the choking smoke out of the room had us beating the air as eyes teared and window openings chilled us. The Aer simply stood there mute and unrepentive.

As far back as my earliest childhood can remember I observed an annual fall and spring ritual that dispensed with all fantasies about the Aer and even threatened to disband family relationships. The prospect of cleaning the Aer's body and pipes always fueled a charged atmosphere with short circuit interactions, slow to die down. I got caught in it too. The impossible trick in my assigned job was to spread newspapers, from Aer to the exit door, that would stay put despite careless footsteps and wind drafts that scattered papers and droppings as Aer parts were carried outside.

The Parlor Stove

The trickiest removals were the intricately hung stove pipes that got unhitched from their bondage before enough hands could control them and prevent dribbling the greasy black contents. Depending on how brittle the contents had become, they shattered and scattered easily. Inevitably housecleaning took longer than usual in an electrified atmosphere.

Though the Aer could be ornery and aggravating as well as cooperative, the times I found her most comforting were the evenings in my childhood and again when I lay on the cot in the log house parlor. The gentle crackle of the fire in her belly lulled me to sleep as I watched the glamorized glow emanate from her isinglass windows and dance on the walls. At those moments I wanted life to stand still forever though I knew it was time for me to pursue my life elsewhere.

That change was followed by others. The log house was replaced by a year-round home with a furnace regulated by a thermostat. The Aer was relegated to the fix-it shop, a chicken coop remodeled into a workshop with a dog kennel in its west end.

During the next two decades the Aer wasn't inhibited by her rustic surroundings or the array of tools. She functioned with gusto when her belly was full of wood or coal. Eventually I returned as landowner and she warmingly supervised repair jobs and my furniture refinishing projects. If she balked or smoked I was irked as it seemed a personal affront, but this did remind me not to take her for granted. As in the past, she warmed me fore and aft, defrosting me after I plunged through winter's snows and frigid temperatures. The kennel's current canine tenants likely thought any activity was entertainment for their benefit. On cold winter nights they snuggled into their bedding when I banked the fire.

During the next several years I neglected the Aer. My preoccupation with other activities didn't include fix-it shop projects. The day a woodworking friend came to purchase tools my father long ago used and stowed in his handmade tool chest, I was shocked at the bedraggled, dusty and rusty appearance of the Aer. With black stove polish, nickel polish, fine steel wool and lots of rags I gave the Aer repeated rub-downs till a semblance of her former luster returned. I cleaned the debris and mouse nests out of her innards and scraped her pipes free of their crusts. I knew she would become unusable rusty junk if she remained in the fix-it shop without the loving attention and grooming she had been accustomed to. She needed another home.

The afternoon she was disassembled, loaded onto a truck and hauled to the Sheboygan County Historical Society this mighty dynamo looked unbelievably helpless and pathetic. Drab emptiness took over the fix-it shop and a tear wet my eye as I watched the Aer leave. She was being retired from work.

She now stands mutely in a corner on the second floor of the Taylor House in Sheboygan amid Victorian furnishings. Signs of her geriatric age blend into the patina that time gives retired furnishings of past generations.

My visits to the Museum usually include a brief rendezvous with the Aer, long enough to whisper, "Remember our days together on my Kettle land?" I wink at her in recognition of the bond we had. A glint in her isinglass windows answers me back.

HAPPENINGS

HOBOS FROM DOGDOM

On looking back, after Blackie's departure for Doggie Heaven aided by the Vet and eased by my hugging arms, I realized that strays like he differed in people relationships from bought dogs who were owned. Strays shopped around when they cut ties with home, sought the anonymity of the land and made their own arrangements for food and lodging. A welcoming would-be dog harborer like myself worked things out with whatever canine came along. The end result became an unwritten agreement between dog and person and had nothing to do with the designated ownership required by a dog license.

The unwritten agreement included discovering and catering to his food tastes and providing sleeping quarters. Blackie could choose to bed down on an army cot or a floor pad in the family room. I gave him his name and secretly endured anxieties that the set up might not be to his liking and he'd look elsewhere for accommodations. His end of the agreement I hoped would include guarding me and the family silver, rescuing me if the house caught fire, keeping unwanted visitors at bay and generally alerting me when he sensed trouble. Blackie added one more job for himself, superintendent of grounds and evictor of gophers from holes in the yard.

He first appeared on the hilltop when the permanent house was in final stages of construction. Like an illusive shadow he lurked around the fringes of the hilltop, watching what went on, sizing up the people. His saw-blade spine and protruding ribs were a cry for nourishment. We set dishes of food near the barn where he came in the early evening to sniff since his presence then was less conspicuous.

One day when the workmen were occupied hammering on the house after a coffee break I saw this scrawny black guy help himself to some sandwiches in the open lunch boxes left on a bench in the shade. When the workmen discovered the robbery they accused one another until they became aware of crows arguing in the tree above. The crows got blamed.

I said nothing about what I had seen.

Blackie got in the habit of looking for the food dish, stared at the house if we were late or he couldn't find it. He remained leery if we neared him, but one day decided to risk it; hesitating tail wags and tolerance of a few pats on head and body gave way to approaching us. An agreement of mutual understanding was underway.

Since there was no issue about ownership between us, blending our lifestyles and free enterprise customs applied to each of us alike. Blackie retained his right to take off for the woods at will. He insisted on pre-bedtime safaris, some brief, some a few hours. We waited up for him. Whether he was out with the boys or on a nature snooping hike we didn't know. There were no recriminations even when he returned long past midnight, just a mutual joy upon his return plus a few snacks for reward and to settle down for sleep.

In time Blackie made himself one of the family, even opting for the front seat on car rides that he loved. He sometimes declined our invitation. Santa Claus remembered him with goodies under the tree and friends learned to include him in their greetings. Some innate sense guided his behavior. He never brought an issue to a head to test who was boss and could impose superior judgement.

Blackie was the first of a succession of strays that found their way to my hilltop and were welcomed. One day as I was weeding in the rock garden Sandy rose up out of the day lily bed like an apparition born there and crept over to me. His low slung short well-rounded body, covered with short sandy hair, brown tinged on tips of ears and leg fringes suggested a beagle mix about three years old. When he wasn't exhausted enough to sleep he was in perpetual motion, so intent on his notions that he made no effort to relate and listen. He bore the earmarks of abandonment and disorganization. Evidently life's stressfulness was intolerable. One morning I found his lifeless body in his kennel apartment.

And then there was Pat, a pert, exquisite, symmetrically marked, tawny miniature German Shepherd, about two years old who responded hesitatingly to women and shied away from men. Memories of abuse seemed uppermost in her mind. As her self-confidence increased in ten months her fear and reprisal toward men intensified. With me she was loving and playful but distrust of other people and loud noises sent her hiding. She liked to ambush and attack people from the rear. I couldn't trust her behavior in my absence. With a heavy heart I took her to the Human Society, recommending a home

BLACKIE

35

with an older woman who had no male visitors, who needed dog companionship to fill lonely days and possessed patience and love.

Another black Lab, about $1\,^1/_2$ years old, arrived on my hilltop, stirring a frenzy of barking objections from my three youngsters: two nine year olds, abandoned at my mail box as pups, and Sally, a two year old German shepherd border collie mix from the Humane Society.

The Lab hung around the hilltop's edge, observing, but more leery of people than Blackie had been. Even more emaciated, Prince's skin sank between bones and his spine stood out like a picket fence. Obviously his errant independence cultivated no skills in food finding. His behavior suggested he had run away from a short-tempered abusive handler trying to convert the pup into a hunting dog.

Labrador Retriever ·Prince

Dishes of food, unhurried time to size me up form a distance and assess my soft talk, eventually persuaded him to allow my approach and touching. I felt rewarded by the friendliness in his dark eyes and noticeable decrease of quivering. He accepted housing in the kennel. He welcomed my appearances thereafter with tail wagging and a wet muzzle that poked me and worked into my hand. An agreement of sorts began, I respected his independence and he retained the right to seek whatever he needed to seek in the woods without promise to return. I prayed that he wanted to return.

Prince became a self appointed guardian of his new home. Without hostility he remained aloof and disinterested toward the other three dogs. He ignored Sally's developing infatuation with him. Every opportunity to be outside she lay down beside his fenced-in play yard, watched him adoringly, and made throaty noises. Hopeful Sally seemed doomed to crestfallen returns to the house.

Circumstances changed. Jim, one of the mail box kids, developed paralysis in his hind quarters three years later and was helped to move on to Doggie Heaven. Prince took over his quarters in the house. Sally's mothering blossomed. Prince succumbed. He even lost his urge to roam in the woods. The two over-sized big black dogs made a handsome pair patrolling my hilltop.

Sally's mothering became more comforting to Prince as an anal gland infection grew more bothersome. The mothering ended the day of Christmas Eve when Sally suddenly became ill. She dragged herself to the Christmas tree where her presents awaited opening, then collapsed at age thirteen. Kidney failure, the Vet said. The Vet's efforts proved useless and on Christmas Day she was unable to move. Prince paced around her, distressed at her unresponsiveness to his nudging. He balked at leaving the room when the Vet arrived to help Sally leave for Doggie Heaven.

When Prince returned he recognized Sally's scent on me because I had held her in my arms as she went to sleep. He hunted frantically for her. My tears evidently spoke better than my words of explanation. He lay down beside me, pressing tight against my body and put his head on my lap.

After Sally's departure his will to live dwindled. His anal gland infection became unmanageable. By Easter week interest and energy to cope with life faded. Pain and discomfort worsened. There was no cure or chance for recovery. With the Vet's help and my arms around him he seemed to welcome being relieved of life and allowed to make his way to Doggie Heaven—and likely to join Sally. He relaxed peacefully but left a long time aching heart inside me plus my great admiration for the way he fulfilled far more in my life than his agreement called for.

It takes just a few imagined yips and rustlings of grasses to make me think that my hobos from Dogdom are with me as I walk the trails on my land.

Chapter VII

THE MAIL BOX KIDS

he morning of July 24th began like any other day with my usual walk down the steep hill driveway to get the mail. My return became unlike all others. I was juggling three squirming month old puppies found in the grass beside the mail box post. Too tiny to be strays, someone intentionally coordinated the mail carrier's arrival with my likely arrival. Adorable as the furry balls were I felt no urge to enlarge a one-dog household to four and raise three babies, a lifetime commitment. I was stuck with a home finding job.

Between getting ready to attend a relative's funeral, setting up temporary accommodations for my new boarders who squealed demandingly, and appeasing my disgruntled Lab, Blackie, I was in a tizzy. Temporary housing on a shed's dirt floor had to suffice – an open sided box padded with newspapers and rags, a dish of water and hastily erected fencing. Hungry pups needed to be fed too.

That night the heavens burst. Lightening, pelting rain and hill shaking thunder made me worry about those three babies alone in the shed. When I looked in on them they fairly flew into my arms. Again, juggling three terrified little bodies I made a run for the house, an ineffective over-sized raincoat draped over us. We dried out together—I on a cot and the three little kids snuggled tight against my body.

Then followed four days of unsuccessful home hunting. The kids worked at it too, successfully. They won a lifetime commitment from me.

Hopefully senior citizen Blackie would forgive me and relent. He bedded down in the house so I moved the little kids to the new kennel built for them on the west end of the fix-it shop. Their apartment had an exit door into a fenced-in play yard. From day one they delegated a corner of the yard for their plumbing deposits and never messed in the apartment. They did their own housebreaking; I simply did the praising.

"J" as in July. Their arrival date decided my naming scheme. Next I arranged an appointment with the Vet. Jim, the largest, plumpest guy resembled a miniature St. Bernard. Jackie, a wiry little miss reminded me of a miniature Alsatian. Both passed their exams with flying colors. Not so for Joey, the smallest, blond and frail. An irreparable life threatening hernia made life expectancy very short. The Vet helped him on to Doggie Heaven as I hugged him in my arms. Tears and heartache for me again when I buried him on the north hillside terrace, my doggie graveyard.

What Joey lacked in energy the other two healthy, rollicking, fun loving youngsters had in abundance plus imagination. They kept my days in flux like never before. Undoubtedly they shared the same shepherd ancestry though appearances differed. Jim grew a fluffy white neckpiece, long tan hair, a white streak on his nose, white-fringed legs and big white feet. He was "all boy" with a "me first" attitude that made him klutzy when hurrying, upsetting water and food dishes. His loud ear-blasting voice announced visitors as well as his own importance.

Jackie by contrast was a smaller build, had shorter tawny colored hair, a coal black nose and three black stripes between her eyes as if she was frowning. Hers was a shrill high-pitched voice that seldom became demanding. When groomed she strutted like a fashion model inviting admiration. Other times she became a cuddly lap-sitter with me. Singly or combined, all overtures of the two kids failed to win Blackie's interest. Besides disapproval of the kids, his throat never fully recovered from irritations left by a stick lodged in his neck years ago. He preferred my companionship; the kids were too active. Sometime after the kids had passed their first year's feted birthday Blackie's condition worsened drastically – cancer, the Vet said. Soon Blackie needed help with moving on to Doggie Heaven. Next, the kids moved into the house. Quiet serenity gave way to a new air of youthful zest for life and adventure.

Sometimes Jim and Jackie functioned with a single mind, other times competition and out-foxing one another was their game. When not following me, tug-of-war tussling, indoors or outside, with twigs, cornstalks or knotted rags, kept them busy. One morning my return from grocery shopping encountered a cloud of drifting feathers as I entered the family room. They had tugged with pillows till the stitches burst. Feathers that didn't stick to furnishings drifted to every nook and cranny in the house. We sneezed for days and I retrieved feathers all year. It was the only time the kids did anything near destructive. They noticed that their fun didn't meet with my approval, so took to their beds, watching and waiting till I seemed in better spirits. They learned to read me like a barometer and gauged actions accordingly.

Generally Jim and Jackie viewed our life together as fun and games, cooperating happily. However, trips to the Vet became a matter of contention and subject to strategies. When they grew too big to lift into the car I had to arrange house call appointments by a stop at the Veterinary Clinic rather than the phone; the kids got the drift of telephone words. Nevertheless, they still sensed when the Vet's car arrived and were primed for flight. Curiosity about what was happening lead them to think they could be invisible when sitting on the stair step just above and around the corner of the landing leading upstairs. Two heads, ears raised, peered around the corner to watch. Meanwhile I blocked avenues of retreat and pretended not to see them. The end result was that they had no alternative but to submit to the Vet.

Toy possession invoked a different out-foxing strategy. If toys weren't left scattered throughout the house they were collected and guarded on individual beds. Jim figured all toys ultimately belonged to him, so he collected and slept with them. Jackie's attempts to retrieve hers were met with growls. She solved that by finding ways to stir Jim's curiosity, pretending great interest with much ado over something. That brought Jim on the run, pushing her aside so he could investigate. Then Jackie quietly returned to retrieve her stolen possessions and bury them among her bed covers.

The kids joined forces when taking off on outdoor safaris, bringing home their trophies to deposit in front of the door: dead mice, gophers and squirrels. Eyes sparkling, tails beating the air, they excitedly awaited my thrilled response. They didn't get it, only my disgust. It bewildered them. A couple more trophy safaris didn't win my applause so they quit.

Their united front put visitors on the defensive on arrival. Jim's vehement barking backed up by Jackie's shrill voice sounded a convincing warning. If I seemed welcoming the kids did likewise. Jim expected a friendly pat from an elderly doctor friend who often visited, and when forgotten Jim sprayed into the doctor's rubbers that were put beside the door. When guests departed he joined the farewells at the door by sitting on his haunches, offering a dignified paw shake. He simply copied our farewell gesture. He had created a "man of the house" role for himself since Blackie's departure.

Because both Blackie and Joey each left a void when they departed I responded to the Humane Society's plea for a home needed by a 3-month-old shorthaired collie shepherd mix. Sally possessed strong mothering instincts from puppyhood on. While she avoided involvement in the kids' play and Jim rejected her attentions, she became more solicitous as the kids aged and developed health problems.

Jackie, at age twelve, was plagued the two previous years with bouts of urinary and kidney infections that reduced her well rounded body to a skeleton. Sally alerted me to Jackie's increasing requests to relieve herself outside. Memory and Sally's guidance enabled her to cope with clouded eyesight and eventual blindness due to cataracts. My heart ached as I watched these changes. Jackie kept her cooperative, affectionate and trusting disposition and was happiest when on my lap. I cradled her with my arms the day the Vet confirmed kidney failure, helping her pass on to Doggie Heaven.

Jim's bewilderment and concern over her absence brought on decreased sociability and activity. The following year at age thirteen, Jim's arthritis in rear hips and legs worsened to the point of collapsing increasingly often. He became irritable. No medication helped. The painfulness couldn't bear touching and assistance. The day the Vet relieved him for his trip to Doggie Heaven, his fighting spirit was gone, he accepted comfort in my arms.

Sally noticed my tears. She reached up to lick them from my face. Her paws laid on my arms as she pressed her body against mine. We sorrowed together.

The kids sleep beside one another in the lap of the land. Perhaps a Guardian Angel thirteen years ago arranged their deposit at my mailbox and jinxed my homefinding efforts, foreseeing the joy and zest for living Jackie and Jim would add to my life.

The Mail Box Kids - puppies - Jackie and Jim

Chapter VIII

THE LAND-SCHOOLED LANDSMAN

"I gotta git your west side stonewall fireplace finished before huntin' season an' snow flies around," said Ed Hurman, a man of many talents - woodsman, hunter, dowser, environmentalist, and stone mason, a self taught perfectionist in all and mostly land-schooled. Silhouetted against a blue sky his sinewy tall frame and gaunt weathered face were sharpened by angles of sunlight. We stood amid March patches of shrinking snow on my hilltop, overlooking a small lake below and rolling hills beyond.

"That's the house where I growed up – like the old one you tore down here", he said pointing to the place across the lake nestled in a grove of trees on a pasture hill. He had built my living room fireplace and now was sizing up the job for a family room fireplace wall. He was ageless, an institution among the locals. I liked to watch his piercing twinkling eyes, always roving and assessing his surroundings. I wondered what he was thinking and what secrets the tightly pinched lips on a jutting jaw held in check till he dared spill them.

"When my folks moved into that log farmhouse I was a year old," Ed went on to say. "Born 1890, fourth oldest of fourteen brothers and sisters, an' no money so all us kids had to hire out. I worked for the folks that owned your place—made five cents a day picken' beans an' doin' hayin'. Been walkin' an' huntin' on your land ever since. Glad you don't object".

The Land-Schooled Landsman

"At seventeen I apprenticed in stone masonry, learned it from my Paw, good man". Ed rambled on, enjoying his

recall. "Started as a mortar mixer for seventy five cents a day - hours went from sunrise to dark. A master mason earned one dollar a day. What's the dollar worth now? Nineteen cents? Our crews built foundations and farmhouses. We quit when snow came. Hunted work elsewhere till snow season ended…Now when do we start your fireplace? You gonna haul rocks up here soon so's I can start sortin' – pretty colored rocks, ones with fossils on 'em, an' fillers too."

Hauling rocks from my back acres depended on how slippery mud season made the firelane hills until they dried out. Jenny, the faithful 1917 Dodge turned laborer, wheezed and sneezed her way up and down the slopes, rocks clattering as we bounced over the uneven terrain. Blackie, my Lab, barked orders to Jenny and me and sniffed out rocks he thought we needed. Ed's enthusiasm over various stones I dumped on the driveway's edge stimulated his running conversation when I was around.

"Think we'll run out of stones before you're finished?" I asked.

"You kiddin'! – Glaciers seeded this land! I already put up 100 fireplaces, stone paths galore an' hill terraces. My Paw did too an' worked me. Back then a mason was a farmer first. Had to learn everythin'—plasterin', brick layin', an' stone cuttin'. No fancy names makin' separate trades like today," said Ed.

One day at Ed's coffee break I handed him a slice of freshly baked apple pie. "Wow!" Ed said explosively, "my favorite! Baked lots o' pies the winters me an' my brother worked in loggin' camps – northern Wisconsin an' Upper Michigan – all virgin forests up there – beautiful. No axe or man had worked those woods. It changed fast. I was hired on as cook's helper, baked cakes an' pies for a 45 man loggin' crew. Washed dishes too, an' towels an' swept out the bunkhouse. A 12 to 15 hour workday that paid $30.00 a month an' board. Soon as I'd think o' settin' down I'd have to haul food by sleigh to where the men was workin'. Then quick start up the fire, serve the food an' git back to camp. Never learned the sittin' habit."

Rarely did I see Ed sit. "I do exercises every mornin', cook my own meals an' take a nap if I git tired. I wash an' iron my clothes too. Keeps me young," remarked Ed with a wink and a grin. I watched fascinated over the way Ed fit stones together as deftly as if he were fitting a shoe to a foot, making sure imbedded fossils, crystals, geological features and colors showed off to advantage.

"Jobs like this suit me fine. I got rid o' my business. Bookkeepin', paper work, an' figurin' payroll tax an' stuff did me in. Started my own masonry contractin' business in 1920. Had a crew, up to fifteen men. Did you know we built the front on the first old Kiel theater? Always worked with fieldstone. Refused concrete block construction jobs…Did you git your vote in today?" Ed asked.

Voting day and I had made a quick drive a few miles up the road to the Schleswig Town Hall, a one-room old time school house where partitioned voting booths along one wall sported the privacy of flour sack drapes. The same pot-bellied wood stove that warmed chilled students years ago now warmed voters.

"That's where I started school at age four," said Ed. "We begun young because our little house was too small for all the kids to hang around. The man teacher made us learn readin' an' writin' without foolin' around. Parents didn't have time to give lickin's – told the teacher to do it when needed but not break any bones. Kids today go to school to have fun." Ed finished eighth grade and after that the College of Practical Experience took over. He married his school sweetheart and raised two sons. He was closest to Len who became his carbon copy in appearance, interests and habits. When Ed's wife died he moved into a one-room cottage on a spit of land projecting into Cedar Lake, a half mile from my place as the crow flies.

As a kid he fished Cedar Lake and kept records on tree stumps of the lake's rise and fall rhythms to help fishermen locate where fish might hide. Cedar Lake was a fisherman's paradise till new cottages disrupted the wooded shoreline and recreational boaters and water skiers agitated and clashed with fishermen over developing the lake for sports events. Years later, after my fireplace wall was built, Ed's records of the lake's natural rhythms weren't accepted anymore as scientific enough to prevent the installation of a well pump to raise and regulate the water surface.

Ed's interest in those water rhythms extended to wondering about correlation with underground water flowage and springs in the area. Like his Paw, Ed possessed the dowser's gift. Both had successfully found wells for farmers. One day Ed started conversation about it when I questioned him as to the source of a damp spot near my fix-it workshop.

"Ever hear about the spring that disappeared at the bottom o' your driveway? Happened when the Town widened the old wagon road alongside your land. Before a well got dug on this hill the farmer's kids toted buckets o' water from there. Some wells was hand dug. Well drillin' outfits those days broke easy. Rocks did it. Your well likely ain't more'n 100 feet an' lined with rocks—the usual—not spring fed. Your land's got one particular spring I been lookin' fer." Ed pursed his tightly pinched lips as if hesitant to spill a secret.

"Have ya heard of Al Capone, the Chicago gangster? He had a bootleg still on your land in Prohibition Days. I only told Len. Him an' me checked all your back acres. No luck. Must have been nearer your house…Supposin' Sunday mornin' I bring a couple branches an' we'll dowse this hilltop an' that wet spot you got."

Several dowsing digressions didn't turn up the spring or bootleg site but Ed did finish the fireplace wall the day before hunting season began and the first snowflakes fluttered in the air. At five o'clock the next morning he, Len, and his two grandsons came up the snow dusted driveway, parked cars and disappeared into the morning's darkness. I cringed at the sound of gun shots throughout the day, hoping the deer outwitted the hunters, but knew Ed's gang came primarily to enjoy the traditional day's excitement rather than collect trophies.

When darkness ended the day's hunt they gathered, as in past years, around my long cedar log table in the family room to thaw frozen bodies and rehash the day's misses, sightings, animal antics and predicaments. This day the fireplace wall was christened with a wood fire and smoke as tales were whetted over coffee and a swig of brandy. Kudos went to Ed, Jenny and Blackie for jobs well done. The fireplace wall was the showpiece of my house and built so perfectly that the chimney's draw pulled smoke straight up and out. Ed produced his harmonica and spun out assorted jolly tunes with all his heart. Next we heard light tapping against the bay windows. An icy snow was falling outside.

This proved to be the last milestone in Ed's career. Heart difficulties put him in a nursing home where he continued to entertain with his harmonica until he was called to build cloud structures and mend the water-works in the sky. Len matches his father's footsteps when he walks my land now.

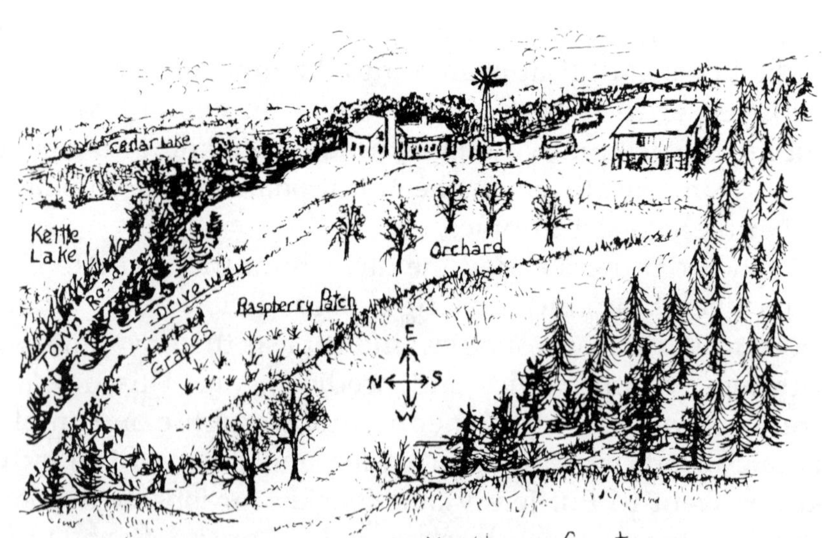

Here lies top of highest hill in Manitowac County

SEASONING THE
SEASONS

Chapter IX

SEED CATALOGS AND GARDENING

he arrival of seed catalogs in January lifts me out of the post holiday doldrums, pumping adrenaline into an imagination that forgets about the tedious and daunting side of gardening and sees only the wide open potential for creativeness in a brand New Year ahead. I find myself flippantly tossing aside the tax return forms that cozy up to catalogs in the mail and then strew the glamorous publications around lack-luster rooms undressed of their glitzy Christmas decorations.

Annually, not until I'm confronting the seed order form itself, do I come to terms with what adds up to successful gardening for me at my age.

The sight of golden cobs of sweet corn on a cover page, freshly picked and steaming on a dinner plate, makes me melt like butter. Luscious red tomatoes fill another page – not representative of the pale tasteless greenhouse varieties I endure in winter. Next I see an overloaded Gold Crop bean bush, said to produce enough beans to fill more than six freezer bags. Seems a good buy.

My gastric juices begin to flow as I walk my fingers through Burpee, Park and Guerney's pages of plump fruits. I weigh the merits of Pipestone, Toka, Stanley prunes and Mount Royal plums. Maybe I should replace the Damsen and common blue plum trees that are dying of old age. Another apple tree would insure a longer lasting winter applesauce supply even though the freezer may be crammed by a prolific raspberry crop. Could I face the store checkout lady for the umpteenth time if I sent her scurrying for more freezer containers?

Mouth-watering garden-to-table harvests detour me to the recipe bookshelf to draft some menu plans with dinner guests in mind. This accomplished, I'm elated at my efficiency but aghast at my list. The catalog people certainly know how to brighten dreary days and wax eloquent over the merits of every item.

I want to feed my eyes on flowers too. So next I walk my fingers over pages of manicured garden paths, neatly lined with floral brilliance and shapely shrubs. In my mind's eye I see potential for improving on the ancient glacier's handiwork that built rocky terraces. These could be connected by meandering paths, accented by masses of rainbow blooms and exotic tall grasses tossing in the breezes. Climbing rock plants could be coaxed to artistically clasp the immovable stone out-croppings. Each year I toy with the idea of adding a reflection pool and the soothing sound of a dripping waterfall.

Startling me out of my reverie is the sound of clicking sleet and snow beating a mocking rattle on windowpanes. I see a snow drift mounding against the entrance door. Shoveling away the white stuff doesn't give the satisfaction of having dug a plant into the dirt but it produces the same aching back and muscles that become less tolerant with the passing years.

I try to retrieve my inspirational reveries but they tend to tarnish as realities interfere. My enchanted hilltop, surrounded by 120 acres of wild Kettle Moraine wooded hills holds attraction for animal visitors who like to fine-tune gourmet appetites on my plantings and compliment me on my pocketbook out-lays. Deer bring their young and rabbits bring their clans. I remember one fall when I planted about 200 tulip and daffodil bulbs in clusters around the lawn, visualizing the "Williamburg look" in spring. Only two blossoms showed up. The squirrels appeared plumper than usual. The lawn looked pockmarked.

Weeds, like wild animal visitors, know no boundaries between natural and cultivated land and maneuver even more cleverly around fencing. Though weeds are said to be flowers growing in the wrong places, my summer battle against their take-over consists of trying to outwit their underground and overgrowth strategy.

By the time I confront the catalog order form with pencil in hand, I'm feeling several shades less confidant about what order to write.

Inadvertently I glance at the catalog pages glamorizing the beauties of the fall harvest, reminding me of the rural roadside stands I can't resist. The colorama of shiny fruits and vegetables heaped high on a flamboyant sunny fall day invites eager customers. Though freed of the labor involved I'm appreciative of the aching muscles and frustrations over coping with the elements that someone besides myself has had to experience. By buying from the tantalizing displays I'll admit I'm missing out on the thrills that I get from smelling and feeling the earth, from watching a seed miracle unfold and grow, from recognizing what bird songs set the work pace and from playing tag with the moving shadows cast by clouds sailing the blue skies above.

The catalog order form stares back at me. My dilemmas weigh out on the side of the happy solution I've found for this aging gardener's horticultural impulses. The joy of creating garden patches exists also in designing and making hooked rugs, a non-seasonal venture. The dreams can keep flowing and catalogs in the mail help organize the dreams.

I call it hooked rug gardening. It won't put food on the table or flowers in vases. Like catalog gardening it is the ultimate in perfection. It means no weeds, no turf clumps to dig, no immovable stones, no bug and soil problems, no four-legged gourmets and no strain on arthritic joints. Once made, the garden lasts forever without special tending, no fade-outs seasonally.

There's no messy turf, just burlap—any size, four feet by six feet maybe, larger or smaller. Topsoil comes from worn-out wool clothing (suits, coats, dresses, pants), washed and color removed. Wild plants (weeds, mosses, tree bark, rock lichens) produce colors I need after boiling out their natural dye. Into the strained liquid I add the wool cloth, torn into strips, plus a mordant (alum, rusty nails, vinegar, or cream of tartar) to set the color in the cloth.

Designs come from fruits, vegetables and flowers cut out of seed catalog pages, then arranged in groups and singles on the burlap, to be outlined by an ink marking pen. Next I cut the dyed cloth into yarn sized widths to hook into the outlined pattern, blending and shading. The hook is a very fine crochet hook inserted in a wooden handle. The yarn is fed from underneath, pulled through the burlap by the hook, making a series of very small loops tightly pressed together.

When I feel the urge to work a garden I simply sketch my ideas on burlap and begin to hook color into the shapes. This gardening is unaffected by weather – snow, sleet, rain, droughts, stifling heat and freezing temperatures—colors remain fresh, no wilting. My garden plots stretch across the floors of my house and have names such as Harvest, Ceres, and Romantique. Birds, bees and butterflies hover around roses, irises, and bellflowers. Cornucopias spill out fruits and vegetables.

On the seed catalog order form this year I listed a plum tree and five sedum, just enough to make me eligible for the "spectacular gift" promised me as a "Preferred Customer" and to satisfy a need to get my hands into the earth, enjoy the feel and smell, and collect some land under my fingernails.

Chapter X

LEFT AT THE DUMP

reezing winds whipped lightly falling snow into a moving dust on the road at 8:00 a.m. one March morning. I turned my car from the driveway onto the back road that in a quarter mile passed the dump beside the junction with Cedar Lake Road, edging the lake's swampy outlet. Movement of a dark rolled-up object where road and dump met caught my eye. I stopped the car.

The dark object arose. It shook the snow from its fur. A dog eyed me expectantly. Ancestry was unrecognizable, perhaps a bit of sheep dog and spaniel, maybe a year or two old. I spoke to him. Disappointed that I wasn't the anticipated person he returned to the dirty scrap of burlap, curled up and buried his head in his tail.

As I drove off slowly I watched the dog in the mirror's rear view reflection. He arose expectantly each time a car passed. A truck nearly hit him as it barreled down the road, the driver pounding wildly on his horn, probably cursing the dog's closeness to the wheels.

The dog stayed on my mind all day as the snow continued falling in spurts. I returned along that road around 3:00 p.m. The brown ball was in the same spot, almost entirely covered with snow. Obviously his owner hadn't come back to claim him and he didn't return home.

I parked at the side of the road. Though his frosted body didn't move, his eyes watched from under icy lashes as I approached and talked to him. He let me touch his body and brush off the snow. After a few tries I persuaded him to follow me to my car and jump in. As I continued talking his whole body shook so convulsively that even the car vibrated.

He was wearing a ragged leather collar, no tags. I wondered how long he had been waiting and would remain there. If he came from a home where necessities had been provided he would have little idea how to scrounge for himself, especially in winter. Tangling with fence lines in search of food risked snagging his collar on twisted wires that could hold him fast to his death. I couldn't leave him sitting miserably beside the road, freezing, and open to the assault of farm dogs protecting their domain from strangers.

Why hadn't the owner cared enough to contact the Humane Society rather than abandon the little guy who was trusting in his return? Unfamiliarity with the area and a growing sense of dejection probably made waiting the one thread of hope. In this instance I hoped fervently that the owner's car would break down and leave him also stranded in the snow and bone chilling wind.

I marveled that my disillusioned unclaimed passenger could trust enough to enter my car and chance my intentions. I told him we would drive around in hopes of finding his home.

If I didn't take this little waif in search of his owner I worried that I would find his shattered body in the roadside ditch. He wouldn't be the first animal landing there or frozen to death.

On this stretch of road in other seasons I have seen abandoned cats. Their owners likely thought food existed in dumps or nearby farms would provide a home. Not only cats but turtles roamed this road, creeping out of Cedar Lake's

Soft-Shelled Turtle

swampy outlet. Many are the times I stopped my car to shove a turtle out of traffic's way. I have seen people, out for a lark and energized by a few beers, aim their cars at the slow moving turtles, then cheer over a hit. Memories of squashed turtle bodies on the pavement made me fear for the fate of the scared pooch sitting beside me.

The next two hours we drove up and down one road after another, stopping at every farm. No one recognized the sad looking chap crouched on the front seat of my car. He continued to quiver though no longer shaking so violently. When I petted him his tongue reached out to lick my fingers.

It became apparent he had not come from this area and needed a home. I already had four dogs and the black Lab who occupied the kennel would not allow a stranger in his quarters. It was too late to drive the twenty-seven miles to the Humane Society. I would need to make room for one more at my place.

Dusk was darkening by the time I drove into the last farm driveway before reaching my own. My neighbors too didn't recognize my passenger. Their oldest of two dogs had just been buried. One dog was enough, they had decided. They didn't resist eyeing, petting, and chatting with my little fellow. His eyes pleaded and they remarked about his appeal. "He can stay here," they finally said, adding, "he must be hungry."

We coaxed him into the house. They set a bowl of soaked bread before him. After hesitating and retreating a few times, his hunger overcame his suspicions and he gulped the food. If no owner turned up he had a permanent home, they announced.

Outside, night winds whirled the thickening snowfall into shifting drifts, visibility dimmed and familiar outlines faded into an all white expanse. More instinct than sight got me home. The specter of a frozen, perhaps injured, brown haired dog body no longer haunted me. He had a home and someone to care for him.

From my hilltop in the months following I often heard the distant shrill barking of a dog trailing a scent in my neighbor's woods. When I looked down the hillside and across the small lake to my neighbor's hilly pastures I could watch a familiar brown haired dog urging the cows to make their way to the barn at milking time – the farmer's helper rounding up cows feeding on the land.

Chapter XI

BEES IN MY LIFE

ne day while leisurely scanning my Kettle Moraine hill acreage I caught sight of a low black cloud traveling with undulating movement towards me. It moved about six feet above the ground, making a deep-toned humming that grew louder, like thunder rumbles announcing an approaching storm. My mind flashed a warning – bees on the move.

"If ever you see bees do that, don't stand still. Fall flat on the ground. Don't move. If you fight or are in their way they could kill you." So began my bee education from a neighbor.

The dense black humming cloud passed over me like a moonless piece of night. I held my breath. Not one bee saw my prone figure. As fast as the bees came they were gone. I watched the undulating black cloud swerve as it crossed the Kettle hollow to a ridge beyond, then disappear among the trees.

"They send out scouts to find a new home – like people setting out to begin a new colony – the Westward Ho pioneers, for instance. When scouts find a good place the swarm leaves the old home," my neighbor said.

Until this encounter I had taken bees for granted without giving thought to the kind of life they lived in the country. Perhaps because I too was newly transplanted, after years of city living, I was awakened to a kind of kinship with the bees. My curiosity was piqued. The ways of bees intrigued me.

Just as my enchantment with my Kettle Moraine acres had drawn me back to put down roots, I wondered if there was something prophetic in the colony's decision to move. According to John Greenleaf Whittier's poetic account in "Telling The Bees", New England's settlers believed a death in the family was cause for a move. To prevent the bees from leaving, they were told about the death by the family who dressed the hives in mourning. The bees were asked to stay, not leave.

An apiarist told me he could tell when bees were agitating for a move. If he set an empty hive near the cluster soon enough he might persuade the start of a new colony right there. If he failed, they flew off to some hollow tree out of reach. He added that bees follow the contour of the land to get to the tree of their leader's choice rather than by a straight line.

I remembered discovering a bee tree one time in my woods because it was singing when all the other trees stood silent. The hollow opening measured about 15 feet above the ground. I'm told that bees build amber colored honeycombs inside. To harvest them the bees must be smoked out and the tree cut down before combs can be dug out.

A farmer told me that when he wanted to keep bees he located such a tree and caught the creatures in a swarm box. The box, made of light wood, had screens or holes on the side for ventilation. When bees smell smoke they gorge themselves on honey, subduing the urge to sting. Next he shook and brushed the bees from swarm box to skep or bee house. It's believed that bees sting only when they or the hive entrance are threatened. Gentle, easy, slow movements supposedly safeguard the bee handler.

When I discovered some odd boxes in a pile of junk stored in the barn's grainery I remembered last seeing them in my grandparent's attic. My neighbor recognized them as Langsthoth Hives, originating around 1860. He explained that the tightly stacked boxes with entrances for bees minimized disturbances when honey was harvested as occurred with the skeps, woven straw hives shaped like giant thimbles.

A memory picture lit up my mind. My doctor grandfather had kept a row of skeps on the west side of his horse barn. When bees were smoked out for the harvest, the bees took off and the swarm disappeared. I saw an ogre presiding, not grandfather – an ogre covered by a wire-like veil draped over a hat, hiding face and neck, plus long canvas gloves in place of arms.

An unexpected lesson in bee keeping equipment developed as my neighbor demonstrated that the boxes contained movable frames, anyone of which could be removed without disturbing others, and set on a stand about 12 – 15 inches above the ground. The boxes served as multi-purpose hives. The bees built storage and brood cells on frames in the lower hive boxes where the queen bee could lay eggs, usually one per minute. The queen "excluder" was put between the chamber boxes and "super" or upper section. It was a screen that prevented the queen bee from entering to lay eggs but allowed the smaller bees to enter and fill the cells with honey which would go for commercial use. The super frames were put in an extractor; centrifugal force removed the honey.

"You kin use them boxes to set up a honey sellin' business", my neighbor told me. "All you gotta do is persuade them bees that's livin' 'mongst the logs in that old house o' yourn to move into this box house."

That old log house, over-run with flowering vines, harbored bees for longer than my youthful years spent with family vacationing there. The low ceilings and walls, honey stained, gave off a sweet undefinable odor on hot humid days. Its essence must have been a mix of alfalfa, clover, and whatever trees were in bloom. The upstairs low ceilinged loft added the smell of smoked meats, reminiscent of storage on rafter hooks years ago. My olfactory senses recorded these odors, tantalizing me with recollections during the years I chose to live elsewhere.

The news that this rooftree faced demolition and a permanent home would be built on the site shocked me. Gone would be the source of my olfactory memories and the comforting hum of bees in the timbers lulling me to sleep. Hardly consoling was the promise that usable timbers would be recycled into a new home, hopefully mellowing the smell of new wood. The bees would lose their ancestral home where accumulated honey and wax had become the mortar that glued logs together.

"Never saw anything like it! The bees sure made some powerful stuff! How do you 'spose they git all that wax laid when they're busy makin' honey?" wondered a workman, shaking his head in disbelief. Next day he brought a bee-keeper friend along.

"Some bees, like people, got over active glands," the bee keeper friend explained. "When they consume honey a wax plate forms on their bellies. Their mouths work it off. Takes six pounds o' honey eatin' to make one pound o' wax. It's the worker bees that build the little six-sided cells where they store honey an' pollen to use as brood cells for eggs. Ever eat honey out o' a comb?"

"Nothing better on hot buttered biscuits smeared with the stuff and sticky fingers to be licked – unless the dogs lick them first," I said. I even chewed the wax-like gum to squeeze out the last drop of sweetness. When finished, I spit out the ball, watching to see if it out-distanced the last one.

Was that how grandmother's sewing basket acquired the little wax balls she used to rub on threads? Or those kept in the pantry to rub on stuck drawers? Did father chew the wax balls he stored in his tool box to rub on saw blades?

These and more questions I took one hot August day to the beekeepers' booth at the County Fair where droves of people were milling around. My questions prompted a crash course in bee education. The facts learned gave me an astonishing and new appreciation of bees, namely: that if it weren't for bees man would go hungry because almost 80% of the crops raised are dependent on the bee pollination job; including production of milk, cattle meat, fruits, and more. Besides that, bees wax was an ingredient in countless products on the market, such as cosmetics, medicines, dyes, polishes, plasters.

The sound of bees is the sound of industry at work, whether laboring on my land or making a relocation move. It seems incredible that mankind is beholden to such tiny creatures for so much of its survival and comfort. If man aimed for as efficient and organized a life, and worked as hard as bees, the economy of our country could certainly benefit. However, since bees tolerate little interference with their single-minded work ethic, they have invited fear rather than respect from mankind. Their role in keeping the human race alive and comfortable goes unrecognized.

I now make a ritual of candle lighting to say "thank you" to those enterprising little creatures. My heart sings as the candle's light brightens the dark side of the day or mingles its waxy fragrance with the balsam Christmas tree boughs on which tiny tapers twinkle in homage to the nativity celebration.

The land speaks of its health and productivity through the voice of the bees.

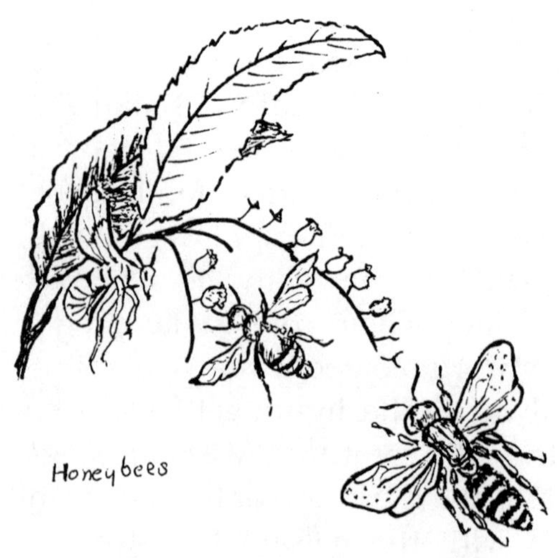

Honeybees

Chapter XII

SCOTTISH ROOTS IN A KETTLE GARDEN

hen I planted the heather – a wee bit of Scotland – upon my return home I had no idea that friends would be intrigued enough with how it got there and survived to ask for the story. Gardeners especially are curious about how a wild Scottish plant adjusts to Wisconsin's Kettle Moraine soil and got the nod from Customs officials. So I tell of the eventful day of departure and the start of a harrowing journey.

The day had been sunny, mild and beautiful as I walked the roads in Scotland's Bobby Burns country, taking photographs and accepting an occasional invitation for a "spot of tea" in a thatch roofed cottage. Before taking my flight back to the States from Prestwick Airport at midnight I walked the beach in a glorious sunset and felt "all's right with the world." I patted my handbag. Hidden in its bottom was a bunch of heather I intended to plant in my rock garden at home – to be a patch of transplanted Scotland.

Little did I surmise that my "goodbye" wave to Scotland as I boarded the plane at Prestwick would not be the last. After this wonderful day I was ready to sleep the night away as we took off across the ocean. Customs had not found the heather in their check of my handbag contents so I was at peace.

We had been airborne about two hours or so when the pilot switched on warning lights and announced over the loudspeaker that one propeller engine was dead and another malfunctioning. Two engines were doing the work of four. The plane would need to drop to a lower flight level. We shouldn't be alarmed to see the discharge of some fuel. We were turned around for a return to Prestwick Airport. Baggage would not be released for dropping unless the engine stress would require it.

A glance out of the windows to check the propellers showed nothing except oil spattered on the glass.

Surprisingly no one panicked. Instead passengers turned to neighbors and interest in one another developed. I just sat there clutching the handbag that hid the precious heather.

I acquired the heather on a local bus trip over the Scottish hills. The driver stopped atop "Rest and Be Thankful," the highest point, to rip an armful of heather from a meadow and thrust it in my arms. The bouquet traveled with me on all remaining excursions, the stems soaked in water at night. For my return to the U.S.A. I selected only the healthiest purple and white heather-bearing roots to carry in my handbag.

As we circled Prestwick we saw the landing field covered with white foam. Several ambulances and fire trucks were standing by. The plane tilted back and forth, jerked and shivered. We gripped seat arms. No one spoke. Tension united us. Our pilot miraculously touched ground with only a slight bump and all was well.

We were interred for the day in a Quonset hut encircled by a barbed-wire fence far out in the airfield. We had been checked out of Scotland. Officially we hadn't reentered. At intervals we were summoned for food at makeshift sawhorse tables. The greater part of the day I was standing in line for the lady's room located outside between the hut and fence, not for personal necessity but to air and water the heather. Hopefully no one would notice that I had violated immigration rules by transporting foreign plants and report what they saw.

By that night the plane had been repaired and we took off. Because ours was an unscheduled flight at LaGuardia Airport our landing clearance was held up long enough for the pilot to give us an air tour of New York harbor.

After landing at LaGuardia, as I walked into the terminal I heard my name called over the loudspeaker system and told to report to a certain desk number. My heart sank. My deed was found out. I could be arrested but I wouldn't toss out the precious heather. How would I talk my way out of this predicament?

At the announced desk number they looked me over and asked some identifying questions. A Customs Officer arrived to quiz me on what I was bringing into this country. I showed him my list of items, heather conveniently forgotten. He asked for my purchase receipts. I fumbled in my handbag for them, heart pounding. Next he pawed through my handbag, selecting a few items for closer inspection. He jostled the cloth-wrapped heather bundle now on the verge of becoming undone and damp to the touch.

By this time I was so rattled and breathing in gulps that I was sure he would notice

The next words I heard said that my connecting flight to Madison, Wisconsin couldn't be arranged that day and I would be put up at the Airport Hotel. A limousine was standing ready to take me there.

As for the heather, it survived five years in my garden. Unfriendly soil and rabbits won despite my care. But the buried stalks and roots have nourished a Wisconsin nursery-grown heather that thrives. The patch of Scotland carries on in its small way on my land.

Chapter XIII

THE RASPBERRY PATCH

"You oughta plant raspberries on this hillside," said Gus, my neighbor, as he rubbed his eighty-year-old back against an equally old Maiden Blush apple tree – and tempted me into a venture I had fantasized about trying. "In the old days the Kahns growed whoppers here like you never seen."

"Why here?" I asked.

"Good ground – chickens an' sheep manured it. Their shed stood here till a windstorm felled it. The Kahns moved away an' the patch went wild – berry bushes choked by weeds. Terrible shame! Terrible shame! I'll fix it for you like it was. My legs an' back ain't good no more but I kin do that much," said Gus. He was talking me into a legacy I was ill prepared to survive or thank him for when overwhelmed.

To prove his point Gus began hitting the soil with a shovel. It clinked against buried rocks but managed to turn up bits of rich brown earth.

"You mean to say berry plants will root in this rock bed?"

"Yep, an' grow like a son-of-a-gun!" my neighbor answered me.

Because Gus knew somebody who knew somebody else that raised the whopper raspberries he acquired for our planting, they came without benefit of a pedigree name. On the far side of the orchard next to the up hill woodland, we staked out a 25 by 15 foot plot for three rows of bushes. Unsolicited "gift" contributions from friends downsizing their gardens added on in time. The berry patch, about 75 feet west of the house and ash tree lined driveway, was reached by crossing the "orchard": 4 pear, 2 plum and 2 apple trees plus a butternut tree and 2 rows of Concord grapes. These had found a foothold amid glacial strata and survived. We had a new stone wall built by the time the berry patch was sufficiently cleared for planting.

My excitement over this gardening venture blinded me to the fact that Gus was planting not for my survival alone but to keep me ahead of future starvation in this country. I had no idea he meant to save the nation with a raspberry crop until I was caught up in the prolific production season.

In my naivete I assumed that after planting one simply waited till picking time arrived. Not so. Almost immediately my bushes got entwined by chokers and crowded by transients – prickly ash, wild grape vines, sumac, burr cucumbers and deadly nightshade. Nettle acted as their bodyguards. Constant weeding became inevitable. Some roots grew by the yard and never got discouraged, pausing in the patch to spring new shoots despite my snipping.

Time taught me that by mid July berry season gets underway unless rain-less weeks in May and June dry up pro-duction juices in greening bushes. That's when the tiny young shoots need pampering so they will promise to survive and produce next year. Mulching with generous amounts of sawdust slows down moisture evaporation and weed entrench-ment, I found out. A poor berry production season proved rare. When it happened I felt let-down by the failed promise and a disregard for my labors.

I eagerly watched early blossoms became green berries and drooled at the prospect of savoring the first red juicy delectables. Somebody always beat me to them! The only culprit I caught was a big robin walking away with berry juice dripping from his beak.

Besides raising berries annually, the raspberry patch housed the annual summer home of an Indigo Bunting pair. I didn't know the location till my sur-prised fingers were grasped by the tiny hungry pink mouths of fledglings. The parents supervised from perches in the Maiden Blush apple tree, prepared to dive bomb me if I upset their progeny.

The greenery also housed vast armies of mosquitoes and no-see-ums that burst forth upon the slightest distur-bance. Their syringe-like mouths aimed to drill into flesh and probe eyes, ears, and nose. Their stirrings irritated bees seeking nectar from late blossoms so they joined the attack on intruders. It taught me to suit-up before doing berry picking: long sleeves, tight-buttoned flannel shirt, straw hat with netting veil and ample bug spray to fight back.

Berry season usually peaks into a two-week plateau during which I find myself no longer the plot manager but a runner between patch, house and freezer, toting 2 gallon berry pails. My dogs supervise my de-bugging and pack-aging procedures, demanding berries as pay even though we dine on berries three times a day.

My kitchen shows off an assembly line of freshly made jams and jells. Crippled berries go into quart jars to become raspberry cordial for Christmas gift giving and serving to holiday guests.

Friends joyfully share in the abundance, either picking their take-home supply or diminishing my stock of berry pies or home made ice cream under mounds of berries. As the frenzied activity subsides I'm thinking I can never again face another raspberry.

Gray Squirrel

That's what a berry picking friend said the day she was attacked by a prickly-ash tentacle, nature's barbed wire wild bush. It must have sprouted overnight when I wasn't looking and nudged into the berry stalks at row's end. Just as my friend grasped a cluster of luscious berries a wind gust came along. It whipped the tentacle into action, hooking onto the rear of her slacks, tearing them as she battled to free herself. With skin bleeding she dashed for the house. Her bucket of pickings tore loose from the rope tied around her waist, leaving her with injured pride and no proof of the labor. "That berry patch isn't to be trusted," she warned. I knew the feeling.

That made two of us for different reasons wishing we'd never heard of raspberries. Timed to oblige by ending their season, the producing stalks turn brown and dry out by late August. Next they're due for pruning and burning, leaving the skinny tall new green shoot replacements flopping in any breeze.

Perhaps to bolster my sagging mood the patch presents me with its special reward at this time almost every year – one or two snow-white puffball mushrooms. Before they yellow I hurry the football sized earthy smelling delicacies to the kitchen, wash them, peel off the rubbery white thick skin and cut the inner flesh into strips to be sautéed. A meal to be savored!

While crossing the orchard intent on getting the second puffball one September morning a magnificent ten point buck deer galloped towards me, emerging from the pine grove north of the patch. Too stunned to move, I gasped as he braked his long legs within five feet of me. Equally startled we had a moment for eyeball to eyeball contact before he snorted, did a sharp right angle turn and shot back to the pine grove.

I wish I knew the buck's thoughts that morning when he veered from the deer trail alongside the patch for a short cut through the orchard. Whatever his intentions, both he and I were regulars in orchard traffic – I, more suspect and entertaining that he, to the dozens of eyes that kept tabs on the comings and goings in that community. I'm a central attraction every time I pass through.

Ever-present suspicious eyes glint from the brush pile beside the Maiden Blush apple tree, the home of a woodchuck family. Its most venturesome youngster sometimes waddles to the driveway but on seeing me, shinnies up an ash tree to the precarious top branches, swaying in the wind. Meanwhile, dotting the ground, gophers sit tall beside their countless tunnel holes, craning necks while eyes assess circumstances. Any dubious action observed makes them dart into tunnel holes only to pop out at others. Unaffected by the gopher's watchfulness, a grass snake, gorging himself on a frog and too bloated to move, threatens me with a fixed stare.

At the raspberry patch I'm likely to meet an opossum mother, pink nosed and white faced, glaring at my intrusion as she slinks along the edge with the aid of her rat-like tail and checks the safety of the little ones tucked in her pouch.

Deer remain hidden in the tall

brush till I go indoors, then bring forth their young to romp and play tag in the orchard. Year-round the deer lay claim on the orchard, pruning over-long tender raspberry shoots in spring, eating windfall apples and pears and snagging reachable ones from trees, and in winter nibbling the bark and greenery of cedar trees at the orchard's edge. When winter snow layers blend orchard and berry patch into the hilltop's whiteness, deer roam freely. Their footprints mingle with countless smaller footprints recording traffic around the sleeping berry bushes.

By wintertime I've recouped from raspberry patch demands and my toil. As soon as I bite into freshly baked muffins dripping with berry jam or jell, or delve into a pile of defrosted juicy whopper-sized berries over a dollop of homemade ice cream, I feel stabs of ecstasy. Winter may be howling outdoors but I'm remembering my encounters in the orchard, bird orchestrations that paced my picking, sunny blue skies and cloud shadows that played with me and the fresh smell of rain washed land. Were Gus here, I'd apologize for having been short on thanks. The fruit of the land puts peace in my soul.

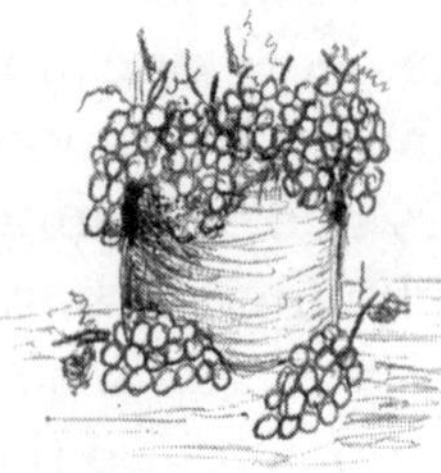

AUTUMN JELL

bout the time summer looks frazzled and fading, I annually get the urge to make Autumn Jell – to capture in it the colors, fragrances and memories of an early autumn fling on my Kettle Moraine hill acreage – the antidote that tides me through winter's captivity.

"Off to the woods this morning! Time to gather wild grapes and apples for jelly," I tell Prince, my black Lab. Joyfully he bounds over the first two hills in the firelanes' path, then disappears into the pine plantation. Thereafter only his shrill barks keep me informed of his zigzag maneuvers.

En route down and up those two hills I see signs of summer winding down like a sagging time-worn umbrella. Quiet sweet scented air lies overall in the wake of bird departures. Tiny starry white asters tumble untidily on the ground. The deep yellow petals encircling brown pincushion centers on coneflowers wean bumblebees from sipping stale honey. The tall mullein's pale green stalks stand like candles in open spaces, dripping yellow petals down the sides. Queen Ann's Lace spreads its white filigrees like a lacy veil over fading green grass. The milkweed pops its pods to send cotton airborne.

"Pods, weed stalks and bittersweet should be gathered now for winter bouquets," I tell myself, "but Autumn Jell comes first!"

At the second hill's base I turn left onto a narrow lane that follows the rim of a deep hollow. Gnarled aged sumacs, weighted down with twining knotted masses of wild grapevines, crowd the path. Picking grape clusters is easy until I opt for the larger, plumper bunches hanging in the thickets behind.

By the time I emerge from the dense undergrowth, prickly ash tentacles have torn at my clothing and scratched bloody lines on hands and face. I've also been besieged by burs clinging to my hair, jacket and slacks.

The nervy hitchhiking burs used me to relocate their offspring in new territory. Yanking them off, one by one, I'm forced to cooperate. The round hedgehog kind, the size of BB shot, became imbedded in my wool jacket. Dark brown oval cockles with wire-like incurling prongs hold on with the tenacity of a bulldog. Stick tights, flat and triangular like glazier's points, pin folds in my clothing. Freed from the grip of the hitchhikers I can move on.

Peepholes in the thickets frame glimpses of my old friend, a lone ancient apple tree in the hollow below. A bit further on the rim path I find the camouflaged deer trail downhill to the tree's grassy knoll. Its trunk, tattooed with rows of neatly dotted lines, showed off a woodpecker's work. No red apples on lower branches, the deer took those, but perfect specimens dangled amid upper branches. I could prod those loose with a fallen dead branch, twenty of them – eighteen for jell, one to snack on and one for Prince.

As I bite into the crisp sweet, bug-free apple, name unknown, I stretch out on the small patch of tall wind ruffled grass. A lone apple tree, thriving on an open woodland knoll, stirred thoughts of Johnny Appleseed. Today in his honor I made a happy September 26th birthday wish. Though born at Leonminster, Massachusetts, in 1774, he traveled far and wide, perhaps passing this very spot as he dropped seeds in his ramblings.

Johnny probably never knew about the apples found on antiquated stone carvings. Or that historical records of Babylon, China, Egypt, and Phrygia (now central Turkey) mentioned the apple. Add to this the apple's references in the Bible, the Hindu "Code of Manu", and the Egyptian "Theogony", a genealogy of the Gods by the Greek poet, Hesiod. Even without knowing the venerable ancestry of the seeds he cast around, I'm glad Johnny brought fame to the apple.

Before taking a second bite I decided to follow Robert Frost's advice. Years ago at an evening of poetry with Robert Frost in Vermont, he handed apples to us saying "You never cut an apple from the top of the stem to the bottom. You cut it horizontally. When you do that the apple is easier to eat and it reduces waste. Best of all, you see the beautiful star shape of the seeds." So now with my pocketknife I made crosswise cuts and munched around the star shaped center. Eleven seeds, a very tiny pile of carpels and the stem were all that remained.

Besides the apple's inner beauty, prophecy dwells in its peel. I remember how expertly Tante Barbara could peel an apple in one continuous spiraling ribbon. Next she'd tell me to throw the ribbon over my shoulder. The letter formed, as it fell to the floor, would clue me in to the man I'd marry some day. My attempts thereafter at peeling a long unbroken spiral seldom produced the same letter shape when tossed over my shoulder. Could it mean I jinxed the charm or would have many husbands?

Little light flashes interrupted my musings – sunlight was igniting wet diamonds caught in a wonderful spider web. It was strung between interlocking branches of two dead aspen trees, hanging vertically like a kite – fourteen inches across, twenty inches up and down. Twenty-seven threads reached out from the center to outer threads, others intertwined, holding it taut. The whole web must have held enough thread to weave a table runner. Miraculously, it was spun in last night's fog from one tiny body. My eye caught sight of at least a dozen more spider webs, none so elaborate. Evidently spiders gathered for a spinning bee last night.

A few more spider webs marked the deer trail up a steep climb to the rim path. En route my stumblings uncovered two fossil bearing stones – halysites or chain coral and the pock marked lithostrotion. Into my pocket went these souvenirs from thousands of years ago, linking me to the time glaciers moved where I stood. Next I spotted an arrowhead. That too went into my pocket, making me visualize the Indians who camped and hunted these acres.

Instead of an Indian silhouetted on the rim path, I saw Prince sitting beside the bucket of wild grapes. Panting, a wet tongue draped sideways from his mouth, so tired he could barely wiggle his tail in greeting – yet he munched his apple eagerly.

"Two hills and then we're home!" I said to him. Side by side we trudged contentedly. A heavy left pocket of stones plus a bag of eighteen apples suspended from my left arm balanced the grape bucket swinging from my right arm.

I rush the grapes, apples and six just picked ripe tomatoes to the cookpot with a little sparkling well water pumped from the earth's depths while the morning's aura still clings to ingredients. Perhaps that's why I see tiny slightly iridescent specks when strained liquid has filled jars that I hold up for inspection in the afternoon sunlight.

When winter's winds howl around the fireplace as burning logs crackle amid warming flames and snow swirls fill the outside air, fragrant Autumn Jell on freshly baked muffins tells me "all's right with the world and on my land."

Chapter XV

TIME TO DYE

Lily-of-the-Valley

'm getting ready to dye," I answered my friend on the phone.

"Getting ready to die? Heaven forbid! Don't talk like that. Life is to be lived!" was her shocked response.

"I've got more preparations to make. How about helping me?" I said.

An audible gasp was her reply, likely thinking I spoke from an addled mind – and not the words of a hooker, a wool dyeing rug hooker.

A glimpse at my kitchen preparations would likely have distressed her further: piles of stained bleached wool strips, a line-up of empty baby food jars, rinse pans, glass stirring rods and four cook pots on the stove. The wool strips when dyed are cut into spaghetti-like lengths to hook into the designs I've drawn on burlap. The jars store unused dye liquid for future use. The cook pots brew the dye plants and then simmer the wool in the dye extract.

The clincher, that I've sold my soul to witchcraft, glares from the assortment of mordants: vinegar, copper, rusty nails, alum, chrome and cream of tartar. It takes the magic of a mordant to "fix" the color to cloth for permanence.

A day of sun and air drenched with songs by the wildlings is like a bugle call to wander my 120 acres of hilly wild woods and meadows in search of dye plants. For that

I need only a broad-bottomed basket with shears, string, some plastic bags and a pocketknife.

Adventure, surprises and so-journs back in time mark my safaris. Discoveries of plants not found before or known ones that relocated add mystery. Like dye collectors in ages past I try to time my collecting needs with the innate dye producing timetables of plants. Some don't jibe. It's their fascinating ancestral heritage that sets me off on mental excursions to earlier eras when dye colors defined the lifestyle, status and customs of civilizations. I feel connected to past times just as I do when walking my land, collecting fossils and feeling in touch with glacial landscapes thousands of years ago. It's as if I'm stripping down the landmarks worn by time and touching its essence. Being surrounded by dye colors magically produced from plants lifts me above and beyond the mundane in daily life. Dye plants live as close as my house door.

As I leave my house with its rock garden at the side I like to think I hear the tinkle of the tiny bells on the sprawled out lilies-of-the-valley plants where the gnomes are supposedly at work doing my weeding jobs. It's the stiff green leaves wrapping the slender bell bearing stalks that I snip off in spring for greenish-yellow dye and in fall for the gold they produce in the dye-pot.

On stones in that rock garden stand patches of greenish-grey, yellow brown or blackish crust-like growths called lichens that give shades of tan when brewed in the dye-pot. Lichens, as pioneer or first settler plants, are fungi that live in a symbiotic union with algae and are easily scraped off. I look for more of these on my stone walls and in the Kettle hollows on my back acres where pioneer farmers dumped stones in an unsuccessful attempt to clear these Kettle Moraine hills for planting.

On a ridge to the east, reached by negotiating two hills and following a deer trail, a delicious spicy fragrance tells me I'll find tansies in a small grassy meadow. Before the flowers bloom the leaves will produce a lovely yellow-green in the dye-pot. If nature times this to coincide with the calendar's Memorial Day week I gain a bonus for the dinner table and freezer, wild asparagus and morel mushrooms, providing springtime was moist and warm.

Dots of yellow among the grasses in open spaces catch my eye – clumps of St. John's-Wort – waxy yellow flowers on stalks 2-3 feet tall. It's the small slender leaves along the stems that I collect for the red color they produce when brewed with an alum mordant. In July the plant tops release a grey dye and in August a greenish-yellow in the dye-pot.

This plant shuttles me back in time to the olden days when St. John's-Wort was stuffed into pillows because it was said to possess the power to foretell the future in dreams.

Believers claimed that the plant's power also kept witches and flies from entering a dwelling if placed over a door. In England, St. John's-Wort was commonly grown in palace gardens to ward off evil spirits especially those most rampant on June 23rd, the Eve of St. John. Hopefully, the plant's prevalence on my land is good insurance at anytime.

Bedstraw, another ancient and famous dye plant I find, belongs to the distinguished Madder family dating back to the third millenium. Its tiny white flowers not only give a yellow color when brewed with an alum or

St. John's-Wort

chrome mordant, but have their origin in medieval legend. It's claimed that because this plant was used in nativity celebrations the tiny white blossoms were tinged with gold as a reward. Practical history reports that the plant served to curdle milk in the cheese making process.

On my land, the Bedstraw cousins, so similar in appearance, include a sweet scented variety that thrives in rich woodlands, another that prefers boggy and wet places and a third that grows at the edge of fields where farmers complain of its interference with plantings.

One of the most beautiful flowers of early spring is easily found along the borders of tree shaded woods, roadsides and thickets where the soil is moist and medium dry – bloodroot. The blossoms attracts pollen-gathering insects, especially bumble bees and bee-like flies. From early April into May the conspicuous broad-lobed green leaves and flowers of pure white petals emerge out of snow-flattened leaf mats to a ten-inch height. Because this plant has been on the endangered flower list I feel guilty when I rob it of one or two roots even after I make sure there are numerous other plants to carry on. The easily injured roots leak a reddish-orange juice that in the dye-pot becomes a rich red, a dye source the Indians depended on.

Box elder trees attract my attention, not for the fibers but for the bugs which when crushed in the dye-pot may give off a salmon color. It's a far cry from the prized reds, Cochineal and Kermes, old timers got from tiny scale insects. The female scale insects lived in warm climates, the Coccidae occupied the cactus in Mexico; the Kermes lived on oak trees in the Mediterranean. Usually in May or springtime, just before the eggs of the female hatched, the bag holding her young was sought. The insects, no smaller than berry-like grains were harvested with finger nails. Incredibly, enough were harvested to dye cloth, paint leather goods, and make medicines.

Throughout the centuries the red dyes were most prized and sought after, mainly because they were considered endowed with life-giving attributes, virility and ongoing life. Even the dead were helped to the after-life with red paints.

As fall sheds its flamboyant dress in tatters, revealing stark skeletons, my dye collecting forages come to an end till next spring. From the sumac's red berries I get yellowish-tan in the dye-pot. Maple tree bark provides purple if brewed with a copper mordant and black if boiled longer. The bark and twigs of apple trees at harvest time, when boiled with alum or vinegar mordants releases a dark yellow-tan. Goldenrod heads produce a yellowish-tan with alum and old gold with chrome mordants.

If I can gather butternuts before the squirrels hide them for storage, I'm in luck. In the green stage the butternut hulls give a peculiar shade of brown in the dye bath. This distinctive color dyed the weaver's homespun material in colonial days and was made into soldiers' uniforms, giving rise to naming the soldiers "butternuts."

Blood Root

Upon return to my kitchen I spread out the day's collections and cookpots begin brewing colors. Gyrating swirls of steam add to the room's transformation. "The sorceress makes magic in her den," any observer would likely say.

"I'm dyeing amid bubbling pots of color – glorious colors given me by the land. The ending of a perfect day!" I say.

"Never mind the dramatics of dying. Stop! It's staying alive on the land that counts," my misunderstanding friend is apt to say.

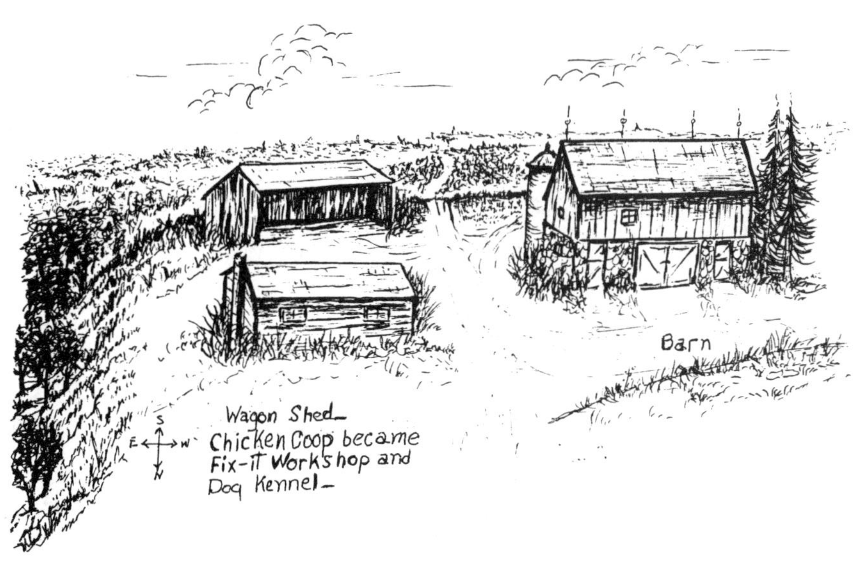

Chapter XVI

BARN GHOST

he idea that ghosts of those who once trod my 120 wild Kettle Moraine hill acreage could return to visit their woodland haunts and the old time farm homestead, now my home, dawned on me when unusual happenings put reason to the test about the barn.

Indian arrowheads and stone tools surface often enough on surrounding land to suggest that unseen hands hold claim on my acres. The 150-year-old hand-hewn barn developed a croaky voice when touched by the slightest wind. Finding barn contents tampered with sans the human touch clearly alerted me that something was going on.

Occurrences like these nudged long dormant notions to the fore about unearthly beings, like the tales read in my youth telling of spirits from times past returning as unseen "presences." It was said that spirits came more often after the sun's splendor had slipped below the horizon and nightfall cast a silvery aura. Their sun was the moon. Mysterious shapes reportedly lurked in shadows, only to vanish if pursued by an ordinary mortal.

The happenings started right after I moved to my hilltop. I sheltered my car on the ground floor of the old barn,

My barn ghost

now cleared of its cow stanchions. Along one wall stood a row of white lime-washed feed bins, plank covered, that held a mess of junk plus a 90 year old tattered quilt intended to cover my car radiator in sub-zero temperatures. The quilt somehow got maneuvered to the dirt floor, standing teepee fashion.

Whatever lurked in and around the barn persisted in opening the Dutch-style split doors flanking the ground floor entrance though I deliberately fastened the latches. Inside the barn a stack of cardboard cartons standing in a corner tumbled daily for no reason despite my restacking. It was enough to make goose-bumps start creeping over me each time I entered the barn.

Could an old rugged barn start spewing out past lives that had caused its existence? Big and little stones fitted together for the 2-foot fieldstone foundation told of back-breaking effort and sweat to haul them from the tightly packed glacial deposit on this hill site. The foundation supported an upper level of vertical board siding, hand sawed from trees felled on this hill. Hand hewn beams and timber frames laboriously pegged together shaped the interior. An outside ramp to the barn's second floor's great sliding doors must have been tuned to the rumbles of wagon wheels and stomping of horses' hooves as wagons moved in and out.

Instead of the sounds of men and animals, the noises I heard were more like moans, groans, swishes, tiptoeing footsteps and occasional squeals.

Across my mind flashed a picture of the frisky revelry long ago when the barn raisers celebrated completion of their labors and hoisted the symbolic pine tree onto the roof as per custom. Perhaps the framework still held the echo of neighbors, family and friends dancing the night out to a fiddler's tune. Sustained by cookery spread out on an impromptu plank table and tantalizing aromas they fed their energy.

Could it be that some of those old souls were returning to check out their handiwork and memories of earlier times – good times but more often a succession of discouraging years when uncooperative glacial soil meant unproductive harvests? Nevertheless, the sturdy barnyard centerpiece still holds its head high with a crown of blue lightning rods across the roof though voicing some geriatric complaints.

I tried to reassure myself that old barns had a right to voice objection to the pressure of passing winds and for the big doors to shudder. Footsteps tiptoeing across the upper floorboards could be wind-blown debris or mice and squir-rels. Reasoning lacked conviction. My senses continued alert and on edge.

No longer able to tolerate the suspense, I grabbed an iron pipe for defense and climbed the short rickety steps to the upper level. My intrusion triggered dozens of sparrows and rock doves high up on the rafters, into frantic flutter-ing. A couple squirrels and mice scampered hastily for cover. A rope, dangling from a post nail, swished on the floor when bombarded by wind gusts whistling through the slitted siding boards.

Nothing appeared rearranged. Garden equipment and supplies looked untouched. No suspicious movement or body took shape in the dim cor-ners. The dreaded and expected encounter with I-don't-know-what didn't come to pass.

Back on the ground floor I glanced around. My eye caught a slow move-ment of some stacked cartons in the corner. Fortified by the iron pipe I poked cautiously. A face appeared. Its black facemask was attached to a furry body. A miniature hand shoved a box aside. My ghost – a one-eyed raccoon. Fresh scars meant he must have been recuperating from recent battle.

For the next five winter months the barn had a tenant. We carried on a "squeaking acquaintance." He squeaked at me and I mimicked him. Often he slept inside the tent-shaped quilt, peeking out cautiously to check my movements. If he took a siesta on a rafter he squeaked at me from there and delighted in pushing dirt down on me. His tracks to and from the barn patterned the snow. In April the barn's heavy silence announced that he had vacated and the geriatric complaints lost their ominous tone.

One day late in May I hiked to the east ridge in search of morel mushrooms and wild asparagus. Considerable rustling in the dense brush caught my attention. Intermittent squeaks followed me. The brush parted and out crept my one-eyed masked friend. For a long moment we eyed one another, then exchanged squeaking greetings and made a couple mouth-smacking noises. With a twitch of his black-ringed bushy tail he bid me goodbye and disappeared into the brush. It was the last time I saw him.

I had been given a priceless gift from the land by one of its tenants, my former barn ghost, when he recognized me.

Chapter XVII

GHOSTLY VISITORS

keptics may call it hogwash but I've come around to thinking that childhood tales about spirits making pilgrimages to their old haunts may be worth consideration. It's the only remaining explanation for some strange happenings on my Kettle Moraine acreage when reasoning becomes stymied. Woodlands where Indians once roamed and an old log house that vibrated with family doings could yet be holding onto the essence of past lives.

Recycling the timbers of that old log house into my new home on the same site might merely have transferred bonds from the past. At times my 40 year old home breathes out the faintest of haunting odors on damp and hot days – hints of smoked meats and the sweet smell of clover honey. Radio and television update my living but when they were first introduced into homes and drew voices out of the air some mortals predicted such magic could bring about contacts with earlier beings.

That prediction popped into my mind when a newly purchased vacuum cleaner underwent a trial run on the family room carpeting and the sound of voices startled me. No people were present. The voices attracted my eye to the television corner. Fuzzy images in modern garb moved on the screen. It happened without my touching the remote control or television knob. Were these souls from the past trying to tell me something? I wondered.

The phenomena repeated itself each time I vacuumed in that room. Telling the apparitions to quit playing jokes on me did no good. Prickles began doing the two-step up and down my spine.

I wasn't about to tolerate such shenanigans the remainder of the cleaner's life, back to the store it must go. I dreaded explaining the problem to George, the repairman, especially since he was wired into relaying anything that made interesting local news. I had visions of my hilltop becoming a local attraction. George thought my complaint hilarious. By retelling my story to others in the store he got enough laughs to shatter a noise meter. Finally he conceded that the cleaner's frequency waves might coincide with those of the TV's remote control. Some mechanical adjustments solved the problem but an embellished story lives on.

That problem was followed by two more that made me think that unseen visitors from the past either wanted to make my acquaintance or assert their long ago proprietorship. Because my family acquired the property in their retirement years and then later I took over, we had no acquaintance with the succession of owners in the early years.

Why, in both instances, would the visitors find electrified lamps a special attraction and for what purpose?

A recently electrified kerosene wall mounted lamp with attached reflector lighted the corner of my family room just as it had done with kerosene in my great grandparent's kitchen. As an antique buff I loved basking in the same yellow glow by which my great grandmother's knitting needles clicked and my great grandfather read to her. One morning I was shocked to find the reflector disintegrated. It must have happened during the night and without awakening my sleeping dogs. Had noise occurred they could be counted on to bark. The arrangement of broken parts puzzled me – some lay among my writing materials on a nearby table; a few lay on the book-case below the lamp; no pieces fell on the floor. Why this seemingly careful manipulation of pieces?

The next puzzler happened the morning after my return home following hip replacement surgery. As friend Evie and I walked from the kitchen to living room we found the floor lamp lit up – all three light bulbs. No one had been in that room for two weeks. Evie insisted that my dogs must have activated a stuck light switch. Or was it a spook with a message?

The intents and purposes of unseen visitors in my house are harder to figure out than those visitors who come each fall and hang around my hill acres. When Indian summer days arrive I can always count on signs predicting "presences" from long ago – signs such as hazy skies, the smell of woodsmoke and the rustling of dry leaves.

According to cartoonist John T. McCutcheon's INDIAN SUMMER feature cartoon and story in the 1912 Chicago Tribune, "the Injuns went away and died but every year about now their spirits git here somehow…See that hazy, misty look yonder? Them's Injun spirits marchin' an' dancin'…See them tepees over there that kind o' look like corn shocks?…Smell that smoky sort o' smell? That's the campfires a-burnin' an' their pipes a-goin'…You jest come out here tonight when the moon is hangin' off yonder hill an' fields is swimin' in moonlight…an' you can see jest as plain as kin be."

So, every fall at twilight I squint my eyes half shut and gaze around my land where Yellowbird and her tribe once roamed. As the green leaves turn shades of red, orange, yellow and brown I see Indian profiles in the leafy shadows and know it must be the tired spirits resting from their dancing. And when some colorful leaves break loose and drift to the ground, I know that's how some old Injun ghost wanted me to know they had been here. To prove it they rubbed off some ceremonial paints that would add color to the land.

CHAPTER FOOTNOTES
McCutcheon, John T. Quote from **Chicago Tribune***, Oct. 18, year unknown, copyright 1912, reprinted.*

Cartoonist, war correspondent, born May 6, 1870, Indiana

Chapter XVIII

MAKING WOOD

ho's gonna make wood for you?' asked my neighbor.

"The trees," I said.

"Yeah, I know, but who's gonna make your wood?" my neighbor persisted. "You gotta have firewood for your fireplace and that parlor stove in your fix-it workshop."

Not until I became a Kettle country dweller did I hear about a custom called making wood. It was men's talk. Women didn't do it; they busied themselves around home. Men got impatient when I asked, mumbled vague words. What was it all about?

From what I could figure out it was some kind of a ritual, done alone or in the company of a few men. It also had something to do with bringing out the manhood in growing boys – girls weren't involved in this strictly father and son thing. It could be a pressing reason for a man to take off on the spur-of-the-moment to hold a communion of sorts with himself and the outdoors. Upon his return he acted revitalized and inches taller as a man.

The women I asked about the custom offered little comment.

Making wood wasn't necessarily seasonal, seldom occurred during the summer, had no set dates like deer hunting but more often occurred after butchering and before the heavy snows of January. They did admit to triggering the event but only if a reduced woodpile and the stove's appetite called for it.

Rural landowners I questioned preferred answering by showing off with pride their systematically stacked woodpiles like gardeners exhibiting prized flowers. In my recollections of early years at Windymare father displayed no such pride in wood gathered and the woodpiles that tended to collapse when hit by the wind.

My non-rural father's uninitiated wood gathering efforts occurred as unannounced disappearances into the woods with Jenny, our 1917 Dodge laborer, and lasted most of a day. Upon their return Jenny's loud asthmatic wheezing and coughing called attention to the weight of the forest she was hauling. When that was dumped, father oiled the antique Lawson engine set into a wooden contraption anchored in the ground. One of two interchangeable blades, one two-foot diameter and the other one foot, did the cutting. When fired up a deafening shrieking echoed through the surrounding hills as the blades spun in a blurred whirl, biting and buzzing logs into firewood and spewed out streams of yellow pungent smelling sawdust.

The racket sounded like Fourth of July fireworks and also clued us in to the prevailing mood of the day. If the Lawson whined down to a wail we knew father's disposition did likewise, and we were cautious. If the engine made ear shattering blasts like a succession of gunfire shots, stuttering and chugging until it began to sing we knew all was well.

Adding up what the locals and father did, I figured making wood began with a disappearance into the woods and concluded when logs had been sawed, split, and stacked for seasoning before their burning.

Making Wood

My neighbor considered making wood as much a part of country life routine as planting the field so he made sure I had some men to do this. He implied that it wasn't decent to be without a woodpile – more than the practical aspect counted. He figured that eleven or so cords of wood stacked to challenge a cold winter was a satisfaction that every country dweller should know.

Harold, son Larry, and friend Len not only made wood for themselves and me but divulged bits of information about what was done. Larry, initiated in his teens by "go for this" and "go for that", was trusted to handle one end of the crosscut saw. His apprenticeship involved getting acquainted with well-sharpened axes, cant hooks, chains, wedges, splitting mauls and then the two-man crosscut saw. That saw eliminated any need to worry about spark plugs or carburetors balking, it always started on cold days and warmed the users while making swish-swish-swish sounds. The faster chainsaw preferred today proves more temperamental.

Loud buzzing and chopping reverberations in the woods help me focus my binoculars on the action whenever I watch from my hilltop. Usually the first victims of the axe, and later the chain saws, turned out to be old dead and dying timber. The greatest challenge, they told me, came from the mature standing tree destined for doom. The situation required careful surveying of the tree's tilt, the impending damage to surrounding vegetation and the wind's wavering of direction. Not till then could a decision be ventured for attacking the tree with the single-bit axe to cut a notch in the lower trunk. Next came the call for a crosscut so as to strike a cut opposite and slightly above the notch – now done by the chain saw.

Initiated sons learned their job was to stand ready with a wedge and maul, and at the half way point set the wedge, driving it to widen the gap and prevent binding the saw. An error in judgement or operation could result in a "hung tree" that required countless maneuvers and lots of anxious sweat over releasing it.

Hauling the day's harvest out of the woods by small truck or tractor towed trailer is a far cry from the previously used horse drawn logging sled that we found rotting in the woods. Very likely it toted the wood that kept the hilltop's log house kitchen iron range fed in earlier days.

The very process of cutting, hauling and stacking wood goes beyond flexing muscles and stretching vertebrae. Not only during the pauses that rest those muscles but also in hearing the woodland's sounds and feeling the air's breath the woodsman's mind can open for contemplation and reading the environment.

Aldo Leopold, the Wisconsin ecologist, has said, "If one has cut, split, hauled, and piled his own good oak and let his mind work the while, he will remember much about where the heat came from. He has learned more than those who live astride a radiator or trade electricity or gas for demanding hungry wood stoves and fireplaces."

Learning what woods burn best necessitates naming the trees. Probably that gave rise to this old time ditty:

"Oak and ash, birch and beach, larch and spruce and pine
Make a fire brightly shine;
Ash and oak burn long and slow, but ash is prime;
Elder, elm and poplar boughs mostly smoke and smolder;
Willow's not a fire's fodder."

Perhaps the woodsman's contemplation goes beyond seeing wood primarily as a fuel and heat resource for survival and he thinks about his forebearers. They needed trees to make possible their livelihood on the land: the rooftree for the house and the comfort of furniture inside (pine, maple, walnut, oak); wagons for hauling; the ash tree to put handles on pitchforks and tools, provide splines for basket weaving and make baseball bats for recreation; the elm tree for making spike-toothed A-harrows to work the soil; the chestnut tree to build fences; the pine tree gave pump logs and sided the barn. Always the leftovers and damaged, dying, sick or felled tree parts landed on the woodpile to keep the fires burning.

His father had taught him to put the white ashes of burned tree wood on the garden and raspberry patch soil so as to sweeten it. His father didn't bother to clear out all fallen and decaying trees lying on the forest floor, believing they fed the cycle of growth and death in the land's rhythm. That rhythm had something to do with the way living and growing things depended on one another. That's what the Indians had told his grandfather. They revered the land and felt entrusted with guardianship for what the land so generously provided. He feels it too but today's pressures put a price tag on wood instead. A dilemma?

For me there's more than heat and comforting crackling as I see wood burning in my fireplace or parlor stove. As I watch the dancing flames I see what some solitary woods-

Making Wood, Cross-cut Saw

men believe and have put into a saying: "every color to which a tree is exposed during its life glows in the fire when that tree is burned. Look deep into the coals and you can find the pinks and violets of the dawns, the blueness of the sky, the burning brightness of the noon-day sun, the angry black of storm clouds, the yellows of the moonlit sky and the brilliant transparency of the stars."

The land gave life to the tree so it could give wood to man and man could make wood.

Chapter XIX

BEFUDDLED NOVEMBER

hat shapes the destiny of a month befuddled by its place in bringing a year to conclusion? The Romans named it Novem, the ninth month. Pope Gregory XIII in 1582 introduced the Gregorian calendar, making November the eleventh month. Its thirty days are caught between October's gold and reds and December's shades of grays and white on black – so it succumbs to drab browns. Its mood lacks October's vibrancy and tangles with December's influences. Its pace is the urgency of Mother Nature's clock so what will be its swan song?

That urgency travels with windy blasts, the reason early Anglo-Saxons daubed it "Wind Month." Others added "Blood Month" since hunters felt driven to do their kills for winter's meat supply. Farmers hustled to get harvests reaped and stored, saying it was "Harvest month." I react to November's variables with mixed feelings: pressure to complete outdoor chores on my hill-top; sadness at the sight of nature's with-drawal from life; uneasiness tempered by moments of delight; and a sense of com-radery with the elements.

On cold and starry nights I hear wind running restlessly like a colt exploring strange pastures. Up in the sky torn clouds are on the move, at night they race across the moon's bright serene face. Remnant beech and oak leaves clinging to trees otherwise bare, rustle like ghostly footsteps from the past. The wind plays with leafless tree branches till they dance and squeak. Gone is the cheery chatter of birds who've winged southward. Hooters break the air's silence instead.

Owls stayed home and made November their convention month. I have heard barred owls in April but they and the little screech owls seem most vocal on frosty November nights.

Screech owls call out at late dusk, not a real screech but a quivery lonely wail, high pitched slurring downward, yet higher pitched than other owls. Great horned owls are hooters.

A great horned owl roosted in a mogho pine tree outside my bedroom window. He voiced a series of gruff-like, deep pitched hoots – four notes or a three series, a slight pause, then a four hoot series, seven in all: "Hoo, Hoo-hoo, Hoo, Hoo, Hooo-oo." A barred owl is an eight hooter who says, "Who cooks for you? Who cooks for you all?" The "all" slurs sharply downward. Have you ever noticed that owl conversations occur in assorted tones – bass, baritone and very low tenor?

About 4:00 o'clock one morning that great horned owl wakened me. Then silence followed. Suddenly terrifying human-like screams came from the ground and catapulted me out of bed to the window. The owl's talons clamped onto a struggling rabbit which he carried screaming up to a branch. The rabbit went limp. The owl ate his dinner, purring softly afterwards. Next morning on the newly snow dusted ground lay some clumps of gray fur and a single blood spot. That rabbits had voices capable of human-like screams amazed me.

Befuddled November

Those first snow dustings dress up November's drab browns, especially if the frosty nights have wrapped twigs and bushes with hoarfrost that sparkles in dawn's early light. Even more sparkly and longer lasting is the rime, born under the small fires of November stars and sprouted over night from frozen fog and dew. Some mornings the mists that rise up from the lowlands around my hilltop create a billowing sea that makes islands out of all the hilltops, including mine. We become suspended between heaven and earth in another world. On mid-month nights meteor showers of Leonid put on a heavenly celebration. Jeweled moments electrify a drab November.

The same cold November night skies that generate such glitter also reveal a prowling hunter in the western heavens, Orion. He's accompanied by his dogs, Canis Major and Canis Minor who wade the fringes of the Milky Way, a wide band of thousands of distant stars resembling a long swath of tissue thin gauze. November's faintly tinted orange moon, immortalized in the song "Shine on Harvest Moon", brightens the sky.

Those reminders of harvest time make me know I'm one more competitor with my wildlife neighbors in reaping the fat of the land. While the squirrels store their reserves underground I'm stashing away in the root cellar: apples, pears, potatoes, squash, onions, and carrots buried in sand buckets to keep them garden fresh. The root cellar is a five by seven-foot fieldstone room in a corner of the barn's ground floor. Screened ventilators, a dirt floor and a sun-lamp bulb, automatically regulated by an electrical system connected to a thermometer, keep an even temperature above freezing. I hope the squirrels don't find out about its advantages over their storage system.

I also compete with the deer, in my haste to pick apples and pears, before they benefit from accumulated windfalls. Those deer I had watched grow up from spotted fawns to yearlings, brought by their mothers to play tag in my orchard, prune young raspberry patch stalks and nibble needles off the lower cedar tree branches. That they and their parents and their relatives would be targets during hunting season distresses me even though I understand the logic of population control. They have my blessings for successful hiding and outwitting of hunters, especially before we celebrate the bounties of the land on Thanksgiving Day.

Those bounties include not only a well-stocked root cellar but also a woodpile that could feed hungry fireplaces all winter and summer memories stored in jars on pump room shelves.

Bundled herbs, hung from family room porch rafters, spread their fragrances into the house whenever the door swings open. Winter readiness also means hanging heavy jackets, smelling of mothballs, beside the door where galoshes stand ready to warm feet as they trudge in early snows outdoors.

November acts indecisive about how to end its reign—whether or not to blur its Thanksgiving holiday with snow or to dump quantities during the last four days to appease December's expectations of a white ground cover. November allows December's pre-Christmas fanfare to invade towns and detract from the solemnity of November's day of thanks for the land's bounties. I didn't get all this activity figured out when I was a kid because I was preoccupied with my own fate. I had been told that at this time Santa's elves were amongst us getting the dope on which girls and boys had earned Santa's pre-

Screech Owl

sents. Not till the morning after St. Nicholas Eve, the fifth of December, would the stockings we had hung on bedroom doorknobs reveal our status. Charcoal pieces meant a bad record, no presents. I was lucky, my sock held nuts, tangerines and candies – it made my transition into the holiday season.

Making a transition to the Christmas season became a custom after I turned landowner. November's last day is reserved for the purpose of searching out the yearly Christmas tree. A whistle and a shout "Off to the woods!" is sure to bring my dogs on the run, barking eagerness for the hike. My equipment is a rope to pull the tree home, twine to tie loose branches for making wreaths, and a handsaw to cut the tree down.

Before descending the south hillside firelane I like to breathe in the beauty by overlooking my 120 acres of hilly Kettle Moraine wilderness, untouched by signs of civilization. Ankle deep snow often blankets the ground. The trees, lined up like soldiers wearing white epaulets of snow, march under a blue sky that's being over-run by moving gray clouds. The only sounds I hear as I walk are the distant calls of the jays, the chuckle of chickadees flitting about and a red squirrel churring defiantly from a spruce tree. Occasional plops resound from snow clumps being shed by overburdened conifers. The woodsy pine fragrance is exhilarating.

More goes on than meets the eye according to patterns in the snow – footprints left by fox, coyotes, raccoons, squirrel, deer, rabbits, and some I don't recognize. An occasional owl pellet testifies that predators are keeping a measure of fear in the hearts of wildlings.

The twisted branches I see on many pine trees bring to mind a story I read as a youngster. It explained that contorted branches were the tree's attempt to hide the hunted. Pine trees naturally grew perfectly shaped till some branches grew bent. The snow and frigid temperatures made this permanent so there would always be shelter for the needy, the story ended. All the more reason for me to choose the imperfect tree, four or five feet tall, to honor at Christmas time. Any irregularities can be disguised by inserting branches to fill spaces, then hidden by garlands, tinsel, light strings and my collection of 1890-1930 ornaments. Standing on a table in the family room, the tree's transformation to splendor makes November's last day seem a special celebration in appreciation of this land's gift.

That day I knelt in the snow to sever the tree from its earth-bound roots and remembered a thought expressed by John Oxenham "Kneel always when you light a fire! Kneel reverently and thankful be..." but I substituted "Kneel always when you cut a Christmas tree! Kneel reverently and thankful be..."

Next I piled cut branches high on the prone tree, tied all together and like a sleigh the greenery began gliding over the snow as I pulled. My joyful barking dogs flattened a snowy homeward path as snow crunched under our feet. The day's lazy drifting flakes consolidated to blur the landscape. They pricked at my Parka and scudded through nodding branches and thickets, making a few clinging leaves rustle like castanets as if in farewell to timeworn November.

November's swan song – a snow white blanket over the sleeping land.

CHAPTER FOOTNOTES
*Oxenham, John. **The Fiery Cross "The Sacrament of Fire"** (George H. Doran Co., New York 1918)*

GOOD TIMES AND TROUBLESOME TIMES

Chapter XX

THE WELL WENT DRY

"Your well has gone dry," said a voice on the long distance phone line at noontime one August day. Five hours later an interrupted Door County vacation week fast became a memory as I drove up my hill driveway. I was appalled to see a huge crane dwarf my house, ladders leaned on its sides and black pipes poked out of the roof. Turmoil instead of picturesque peacefulness reigned. Was the Cedar Lake well pump the root of this mess?

My well site booboo was made on the ill-founded advice of the contractor. At the time the house was built on the log house site, he incorporated the original well in the basement pump room. He argued convenience and easy maintenance. Directly above the well were built-in trap door openings on first and second floors and on the roof "in case" we ever wanted to remove the well pipes. No state building codes against this existed at the time.

As I entered the family room door I faced into muck dripping well pipes that stretched up and out through the roof into the blue sky above. Many footsteps had already tracked muck over the carpeting.

"Nothin's wrong with those old well pipes workin' – you just ain't got no water anymore in that well. You gotta git a new well dug – and that can't be in here." I was told. The well driller would come in a couple days but it would take time to find water in this glacially packed Kettle Moraine hill and might cost a fortune.

My worst fears about this happening took root about ten years earlier when a well and pump were installed at Cedar Lake, a half mile from my property. The sputter and churn bit drilling outfit worked there over six months setting nerves on edge among nearby property owners and giving rise to complaints about water pressure problems in some wells, mine included, in the following years.

What started all this trouble in the first place was the greatly increased use of Cedar Lake for water sports and the wish to enlarge the water surface by pumping water into the lake. Heated controversy raged between fishermen protecting prime fishing territory and new lake cottage owners. They wanted the lake to sustain a constant yearly water elevation of 97 feet above sea level for water sports. Fishermen wanted a weedy shoreline for fish habitat and feeding plus quiet undisturbed waters. Lake depths ranged from 4 to 28 feet despite the annual cycles of rising and falling water levels, natural evaporation and rainfall amounts giving minimal variations.

The water levels were predictable, occurring yearly in cycles, documented by the lake's longest resident cottage owner, Ed Hurman. He maintained that nature's rhythms would continue regardless of well installation, a costly operation into the future and interference for fish habitats. Though a respected self-taught conservationist, Ed's opinions were pooh-poohed.

Proponents out-voted the fishermen and decided to finance the well and its maintenance, electing to form a Sanitary District of all lake property owners who would pay an annual levy.

My property lay outside but adjacent to the District, close enough for interference with the underground water vein feeding my well. I contacted the Department of Natural Resources (DNR) who were assisting and approving the lake project. I was told not to worry, the Cedar Lake well was too deep to affect it.

During the months that the well drilling proceeded at Cedar Lake local newspapers printed frequent reports on progress. Because my hill at 1,047-foot elevation came from the same glacial action thousands of years ago that created the surrounding hills and the lake, I watched reports closely.

First reports stated that well drillers averaged 5-10 feet per day. This slowed to 2-3 feet due to large boulders, some four feet in diameter, instead of the anticipated limestone. Engineers estimated glacial drift made up the top 125 feet of soil. A Niagara limestone layer, estimated to run from 125 feet below the surface to a depth of 525 feet followed. Then came a layer of Mequota Shale, extending to 825 feet. Galena-Platteville limestone made up the remaining strata down to the 1150 level – the possible well depth.

My apprehensions increased on reading further reports. The Cedar Lake well was expected to pump 500 gallons of water per minute. Estimates claimed that two months of pumping would produce 45,600,000 gallons of water to raise the 139-acre lake one foot. Where would all that water come from?

Reports on estimated costs made me count dollar signs instead of sheep at bedtime. If the well performed satisfactorily on drilling and testing, costs ranged from $17,400.00 to $34,262.00 if extended to the 1150 level. Equipment costs alone ranged from $10,000.00 to $15,000.00. Considering the composition of my hill and the possible greater depth before locating water would my costs approach these?

In the decade that followed the Cedar Lake well's completion and operation my well had more pressure problems. Then came the August day when it went dry.

Three days later at 7:30 a.m. the giant well drilling rig squealed and maneuvered its way up my steep wooded driveway, leaving a mess of torn branches and leaves behind. Trucks piled high with equipment and workers made my hilltop as crowded as a parking lot on flea market day.

Selecting a drill site arbitrarily was accomplished quickly without benefit of technical devices or my dowser friend's recommendations. Guess work, they admitted. State Codes specified distances from the house, underground fuel tanks and septic systems. Therefore, the site lay eight feet from the southwest corner of the house beside the driveway.

Besides the risk of not finding water, the footings of the field stone fireplace along the west wall could be unsettled by the vibrations and digging of a seven foot deep trench past it to reach the pump room on the other side. Copper water pipes and electric wires laid there would connect the well and motor to the set-up in the pump room, passing through a hole in the foundation.

Day One of well drilling: gravel and stones showered out continuously.

Day Two: More gravel and stones spewed out. Boulders slowed progress. Doubts about site suitability were announced. Concussions shook the earth each time drills made pulverizing bites. The house rattled. I prayed for water, not oil.

Day Three: The lovely green lawn beside the house lay buried under 3 inches of cement-like gravel. Rumors of drilling problems brought a series of on-lookers who speculated on the outcome, passed out advice freely about ideas for lawsuits against the Cedar Lake project and DNR. The unanswered question remained, how could we prove my well problem was the result of the Cedar Lake pump's draw on my water vein?

Day Three late afternoon: The drill reached 210 feet and

the first signs of water. The on-lookers cheered. More drilling and the flow improved by evening.

Day Four: The 7-foot deep ditch was dug past the fireplace and it didn't fall. Water pipe and electrical connections finally brought water back into the house after a week of hauling water by car in buckets and recycling the used supply. At a depth of something over 300 feet the new well's water flow was pronounced satisfactory and water tested safe for drinking but high in iron content.

By the time the mess was cleaned up, bills paid, grassy lawn recovered and I began to take the new well and pump's efficiency for granted I thought my troubles were over. Not so.

One-day radio and newspapers carried alerts to well owners about PCB's found in common well pumps. A national health alert urged removal of well pump models, pre-1980, submersible two-wire, not three-wire, pumps. Three manufacturers were named. My pump was a submersible made by one of them. The installation literature gave no clue as to the wire model or manufacture date.

Further alerts stated that DNR and industry officials agreed the pumps were harmless unless PCB's leaked from the pump's capacitor into the motor oil and then into the water system. What was a capacitor? Where located? Pump replacement costs, they said, ranged between $500.00 and $2,000.00.

I felt on the brink of another disaster – contaminated house pipes, health hazards and depleted bank account.

Where were my answers? Worsening my predicament was the news that after the heart attack death of my plumber, Gordon, all his records had been destroyed. My skimpy information about the well installation proved insufficient for the Department of Natural Resources to clarify my questions. My last try was the well drilling company. Due to time lapse they doubted having kept any records on my well installation. Seven anxiety-ridden days later they returned my phone call. Good news! Mine was a three-wire installation that used no oil lubricant, hence no PCB contamination possible.

Suspicious but unprovable, the Cedar Lake well pump drained the water vein that fed my well, generating a nightmare chain of events that leaves me anxious today about the future. As long as the Cedar Lake well pump continues operation am I doomed to a repeat catastrophe? Land locked secrets lie buried in my glacial under-pinnings and the land won't tell.

CHAPTER FOOTNOTES
The Sheboygan Press 12/30/71 **"Well Drilling Project Initiated To Raise Cedar Lake Water Level"**

IBID 5/18/72 **"601 Foot Well May Raise Cedar Lake Water Level"**

Manitowoc Herald Times 7/7/72 **"Cedar Lake Team Using Well Pump To Save Resources From Disappearing"**

IBID 1/9/73 **"Plan Resumption of Pumping at Cedar Lake, Concerns on Environment"**

Kiel Record 1/18/73 **"Citizens Form Sanitary District To Help Preserve Cedar Lake"**

IBID 6/7/73 **"Cedar Lake Well Dedicated"**

Chapter XXI

WHAT THE DOWSER'S ROD DIDN'T FIND

he sound of a rattling car coming up the driveway made me turn around in time to see a rust colored Pinto and Ed Hurman unscrambling his near six-foot lanky frame from a crouched position, holding high two sticks – our dowsing rods. I was to be initiated. We hoped to unlock some water secrets on my Kettle Moraine acreage and locate the spring site where a notorious Chicago gangster had set up a booze making still long ago. This May Sunday morning our venture seemed blessed like the land as we listened to the distant bells of the Louis Corners Church calling the congregation together.

I had told Ed about a persistent wet spot beside the fix-it shop, shaded by Ostrich ferns and an apple tree. If it hid a spring I envisioned digging a pond whose overflow would become a gurgling stream meandering past the east side of the house and through the rock gardens on the north hill slope. Ed had many talents – a skilled fieldstone mason, a wise outdoorsman, a respected dowser. He offered to teach me the magic of the dowser's wand.

"Willow forks work better than apple or witch hazel that some use" he explained, handing me a branch measuring approximately the width of a little finger, about two feet long with two prongs. "Take the prong's end in each hand, palms up, point the crotch straight up. Now start walking", he said, adding "if we pass over running water under the sod, any depth, the stick can dip so forcefully it'll be hard to hang onto."

All morning we criss-crossed the hilltop, but no bobbing wand. Ed's rod moved at the fix-it shop's wet spot and again near the ramp at the barn's rear, too lightly to be significant, Ed said. He shook his head, "Wet but not spring fed. No flowing water. Just low spots that don't drain dry." My rod quivered from my excitement rather than a mystical attraction to the sub soil water-works. My fantasy of a pool and a babbling brook had no future.

We settled on a coffee break back at the house. Ed and I paged through two of Kenneth Robert's books, **Henry Gross and His Dowsing Rod** and **The Seventh Sense**. Henry Gross, a real person, possessed the phenomenal ability to find water for a thirsty world – for organizations, the military, industry and governments. One proof is a bronze plaque on a school in Hollis New Hampshire that reads: "The water supply of this school flows from the veins dowsed on a map in Kennebunkport by Henry Gross and Kenneth Roberts November 7, 1951, proved in Hollis November 8, 1951." It listed the names of five local people.

Roberts was known to successfully locate a water vein by just working over a map without being on the site. He considers dowsing a seventh sense that all people don't have. Science can't prove why. He defines it as "the working of a dowsing rod or its equivalent, in the hands of a competent dowser on flowing underground water: not any underground water, not on motionless deposits, such as are punctured by so-called artesian wells, but on water moving in underground rivers, sheets, veins and domes." Before geologists took over, guiding or deriding dowsers, dowsing was a respectable profession with a history over hundreds of years for producing countless working wells.

Ed got his dowsing start during the 1920's, Prohibition Days, a time when scouts snooped around the countryside looking for quality water to use for bootlegging stills. It was all very hush-hush. "You know, don't you, that Al Capone, the Chicago gangster himself checked out your water and arranged to hide a still on your land" Ed had said one day when building my fireplace wall.

"Let's make another try," said Ed, ending our coffee break. This time we tried to form a mind-set such as Capone must have had when he chose the ideal still site: easy access to spring water, no near neighbors, an unobtrusive exit route for transporting the brew, normal looking surroundings. That placed it in the vicinity of the barn. We figured that an unsuccessful pioneer farm family might have welcomed some extra cash by shielding the operation.

As often as we retraced our steps around the rear of the barn it never occurred to us to investigate further the source of dripping water inside the barn's ground level or the curious feature's of the ramp at the barn's rear. Time revealed nothing new.

When I was in the throes of selling my property five years ago an architectural historian came to evaluate the old hand hewn barn. He became intrigued by the unusual features of the barn's rear ramp. He noted that the huge sliding doors at the second floor level could accommodate wagons, trucks, or large equipment without activity visible at the barn's front and driveway. Unusual was the purposeless three-foot square cement slab, bearing iron handles, imbedded in the soil at the ramp's top west side. The slab seemed in an impractical location for tying horses. It appeared to be a lid, too heavy for manual removal.

Beneath the barn's second floor doorway and projecting through the two-foot thick fieldstone foundation into the ground floor interior were two pipes that dripped water constantly. The water was clear, odorless, and constant, rain or shine. I was told it came from a cistern that collected rain water. How could that be if there were no rain gutters or downspouts on the barn to funnel water to the cistern? Cistern water was usually stale, hardly safe for watering livestock. Furthermore, the barnyard windmill had pumped fresh water into drinking troughs for livestock use. The more I puzzled over inconsistencies, the more I began to suspect the existence of a spring.

Could it be that the ramp's cement slab was the entrance to a chamber under the ramp and had housed the bootlegging operation? Between the ramp and the southeast corner of the barn, where a topless silo stood, lay a small stretch of caved-in cement that at one time might have covered an extended passageway between barn and silo and ramp. An accumulation of debris, wild grapevine entanglements, rocks and wires defied investigation until major clean up could be done.

The pending sale of the property didn't allow time to check out my findings further. I would leave an unsolved mystery for future owners. I wished Ed could descend from the wild blue yonder where he went to live twelve years ago with his dowsing rod. We had come so close to discovering this site. It met all the qualifications we figured Al Capone wanted for a still location on land I subsequently acquired.

Four years after my hilltop property had been sold, it was resold. The new owners had a son who became enough intrigued by the ramp's cement slab to use tractor power to jiggle it loose. Underneath was a large room, a dirt floor and signs of a spring. Until further investigation can be done we find ourselves speculating about what sorts of skeletons will be found, what tales the site can tell, and what water secrets the land may reveal.

CHAPTER FOOTNOTES
Roberts, Kenneth **Henry Gross and His Dowsing Rod**
(Doubleday & Co. Inc. 1952)

Roberts, Kenneth **The Seventh Sense**
(Sequel to HENRY GROSS) (Doubleday & Co. Inc. 1953

Chapter XXII

TROUBLE ON MY LAND

ust as soon as I bask too long in the arms of complacency, enjoying the good life on this Kettle land, my senses get ticked off by a feeling of foreboding. Something tells me that both man's foibles and nature's temperament have their say-so too. "Brace yourself! Expect the unexpected!" I tell me.

That sense of foreboding gnaws at me when weeks of intense dryness set in, like one September when everything on the land became a tinderbox. Radio and TV sounded warnings. Outdoor fires were banned. I began sniffing the air on walks with my dogs while they took care of the animal scents. One day I smelled smoke. It intensified along the south end of my hilltop. Was it my imagination or actually a slight haze drifting from the south?

I focused binoculars on my far back acres and the Nager farm beyond. A gray spiral seemed to be rising from the barn's vicinity. Had they defied brush-burning restrictions? The smoke darkened. Did I see red streaks? My nose smelled burning wood.

I raced to the house, phoned the fire department, and hoped the fire wouldn't leap into my pine plantation and ignite the pine needle carpeting. From there it could quickly engulf the several hundred surrounding forested acres.

By day's end only a smoky haze lingered over the land. Neighbors had rallied to extinguish the blaze on the Nager house roof. Volunteer firefighters from three fire trucks concentrated on the flames consuming the newly remodeled barn. That evening neighbors pitched in to milk cows, shared their cut feed supplies, brought lumber and assisted with temporary repairs. An electrician friend installed enough new wiring for temporary lights.

Hero praise went to Ron Nager's Blue Heeler herding dog for saving twenty-nine head of cattle and one skittish bull trapped in the barn, slated to be so much barbeque. She entered the flaming barn and led twenty-seven cows safety outside, then returned to bring out the other two heifers and the ornery bull.

Ron's loss included some 142 laying hens in an adjoining chicken and hog shed, a valuable two year old bull, a calf, some eighty tons of hay and straw, a new combine and a just purchased hay chopper. The Nager's saw their good life disintegrating in a few hours because some sparks from their house chimney had gone astray.

Too distraught to weigh gains against losses Ron opted to sell, leave farming for city work. The good life on the land lay tarnished in the rubble and not in what had been saved. That nature would soon forgive the blackened mar among his unharmed plantings, and regreen the land, was immaterial. Surveying the twisted metals in the wreckage of the once well equipped dairy barn his wife said, "We don't feel much like going on after all our hard work and savings lie out here in rubble. We've got three children and a new baby to think about". In the tragedy they had lost their faith in nature's cooperative powers and their own resourcefulness.

Some months later when surveying springtime's eruptions of leaves around my hilltop my same apprehensions flared up when I noticed a spiral of smoke to the east beyond the high ridge that marked my property line. It arose from a large parcel of wooded land recently purchased by a Chicago couple seeking a rural life away from city stress. I phoned them. No answer. I phoned the next neighbor who later reported that the Chicago man was burning brush in an open wooded area and got his first lesson in how to live with his environment.

When the smell of wood smoke at dusk one day was accompanied by the uncanny beat of a boombox somewhere in my pine plantation to the south of the hilltop I knew Indian ghosts weren't holding a pow-wow. With the dogs at my heels we set off to investigate. Car tracks matted the grass, from a cut barbed wire fence on my boundary line abutting the County Park to a knoll amid pine trees. On the knoll stood a tent, a camper truck, a cracking campfire and the boom box. Two reclining fellows, unperturbed by my arrival, scoffed at being reminded of their "No Trespassing" violation, the fire hazard and my orders that they leave. Not till I signaled my dogs to threaten them did they depart.

Also blind to the "No Trespassing" signs are hunting season's gun toters who disregard asking landowner permission. The same dry leaves and pine needles that soften their footsteps can catch a cigarette ash that smolders into a flare-up later. Also, in their zeal to flush out deer I occasionally met those hunters criss-crossing my hilltop, moving between buildings and clumps of trees with guns pointed, ignoring my orange jacketed presence and barking dogs. A spent bullet and a punctured house window have explained my fright. Hence, my reluctance to give hunting permission.

My fright soars if late at night the smell of wood smoke drifts up the north slope of my hilltop. Between May and October youthful revelers periodically gravitate to a secluded site off the town road below, where woodland levels off to the lake. Unseen from the road but visible from my hilltop house are their campfire parties and carousing.

Damp leaves that mat the forest floor are not immune to smoldering long after the party has dispersed. The sight of a cruising county police car sends the revelers scurrying.

Besides man's misguided actions, it seems nature gets into the act too. Storms. Dependable forecasters are birds gorging themselves at the feeders and my dogs, pacing, panting and checking hiding locations. The arrival of thunder reverberations that rattle windows, blinding lightening flashes accompanied by noisy crackles, put nerves on edge. I worry about fire from strikes. If rain follows I assume it will douse any burn.

One such onslaught in August proved terrifying. Two sixty-year-old giant spruce trees, 26 feet from the front porch near the driveway's edge were the target. The day had dawned with a reddish sky. Motionless air turned hot and sticky. Clouds, some anvil shaped, shading from gray to black, mounted in the northwest.

By early afternoon distant thunder rumbles grew louder. Lightening streaks illuminated faraway black clouds headed towards us. Suddenly a strong wind blew out of the over-riding blackness and whipped trees into wild dances. Then the storm hit with fury, one thunderclap after another, punctuated by blinding lightning. Next came an ear-splitting crack. The house trembled. Windows rattled. Dishes on shelves clinked. A lightning flash blotted out all window views for uncountable seconds – an eternity.

I watched transfixed at the kitchen window while my dogs hid behind a door under a kitchen shelf and yipped. I saw a fireball, big as a basketball, emerge from the spruce tree's mid section. It rolled down the trunk, then along the driveway passing the kitchen windows and headed for the barn. It didn't disintegrate til it touched the wet grass.

The blue spruce tree was now on fire at mid section. Thanks to a deluge of pelting rain the fire didn't reach to the tree's twin and was extinguished. The rain made a gushing river out of my driveway, wiping out the charred trail left by the fireball. The spruce thereafter bore the storm's souvenir, a twelve-inch round black scar and a three-inch wide black band down its trunk.

Too wounded to heal, the spruce tree tolerated fall's windstorms but winter's gusty blasts and weighted snows toppled the tree with a mighty crash in January. It fell alongside the house making eerie screeches like cries of desperation from an aged monarch. After spring warmth cleared away the snow, the tree was sawed and the wood stacked to season before fireplace burning. The tree's twin has rounded out and still stands tall.

Trouble on my land, be it of man's making or nature's wrath, can shake me up but not uproot my footing in the land, I've discovered. My claim of possessing the good life seems to come from a kind of symbiotic relationship with the land and its elements, balancing trouble with rewards and measuring with whatever degrees of ingenuity I can contrive. It's like taking a hike in my woods where it's easy to get lost – lost enough to find myself.

Chapter XXIII

LIGHTNING RODS AND BEN FRANKLIN

ne morning Prince, my Lab, and I were interrupted on our walk by the tinny rattle of a metal truck bouncing over the recently rain-gutted hill driveway. Prince swung around with mounting agitation to investigate the intruder. A tall skinny man, aged about 30, unshaven and wearing wrinkled faded overalls emerged from a rusty blue truck. Remaining in the truck, an unrecognizable young man slid down in the seat so his head was barely visible. The tall fellow greeted me cheerily and announced that he was a lightning rod inspector. I knew there was no such job in the state. I became suspicious about his intentions.

"What kind of inspections do you do?" I asked.

"I'll need a tall ladder to get up on both your barn and house roofs to inspect those rods. Do you know those colored glass balls don't give much protection? They need to be changed. New ones work better," he said.

"Why?' I asked.

"Yours are worn out. I also want to see how they are grounded and if inside your barn and house they are properly attached," he answered and began walking toward my barn. Meanwhile Prince stood close beside me growling under his breath as he eyed the man intently. I knew Prince too recognized him as a fake, up to no good.

I decided to play the man's game and try to outsmart him rather than to risk a possible attack. The fellow in the car was probably his assistant. Fortunately both house and barn were locked.

"All inspectors have licenses," I said. "I'll need to see yours before we proceed further." He said his was in the truck and went to the rear carrier of the truck which was empty except for a dirty worn catalog that pictured lightning rods among other accessories for outside buildings. He paged through the booklet and flashed an order page past me saying, "the license is here."

"Why isn't that license like the one my electrician and other inspectors carry?" I asked, sounding innocent.

He eyed me closely as I explained that my electrician and carpenter both inspected these lightning rods last week and assured me all was satisfactory.

The car-seated accomplice had been watching us, turned his head and slid lower down on the seat. The lightning rod inspector moved around nervously and finally said, "I'll go to get my professional license and come back later."

He jumped hastily into the truck, zoomed fast around the turn-around in front of the barn and tore down the driveway with his noisy rattling truck. I phoned the police who thought the man would approach others in the area and needed watching. The fellow never returned and that was the last I heard of him around here.

"Whew!, Ben Franklin, who'd have thought I'd get into a tight fix because the famed offspring of your 1752 invention were standing a-top my house and barn on Wisconsin Kettle Moraine land?

Little did I realize during the years I lived in Ben Franklin's hometown, Philadelphia, Pennsylvania, how much of the heritage that he left I had absorbed and which would in turn affect my life on this Kettle Moraine hilltop. My walks past his life-like statue on the University of Pennsylvania campus or waving at his seated figure in front of the Post Office personalized his accomplishments for me. He was responsible for the existence of eight lightning rods on my land, four on the log house roof and four on the barn.

Back in 1752 Ben's fascination with electrical phenomena led him to fly kites in thunderstorms. He found out that the electrical nature of lightning happened when positive and negative charged particles separated in thunderstorms, due probably to the action of water and ice particles in clouds hit by cosmic rays. This triggered lightning strikes from cloud to earth as forked branches. If lightning remained in the cloud it was known as sheet lightning.

The accompanying sound of thunder resulted from the rapid expansion of heated columns of air that passed through the cloud, according to Ben. These reached exceedingly high temperatures that forced expansion which formed the shock waves creating the thunder clap. Knowing this didn't help in any way to ease my fears when the height of my hilltop, plus tall trees and the barn seemed to attract the electrical displays. I wonder if Ben could have done any more about that beyond his invention of the lightning rod?

As soon as Ben proved that lightning was a form of electricity he got the idea, when experimenting with a metal key attached to the kite string, that metal rods installed on top of buildings and connected by thick wires to the ground made lightning choose to pass through metal and travel to the ground without harming a building. He reasoned that when lightning strikes from cloud to earth it seeks out the tallest target and if this is a metal rod its low electrical resistance attracts the strike. His first test was successfully tried out with a rod on top of Philadelphia's historic Christ Church.

The success of the theory persuaded the colonies and King George III in 1776 to order lightning rods. The King installed the blunt ends on his palace. By 1782 Philadelphia sported 400 lightning rods.

No sooner were lightning rods invented as protection then their decoration was promoted as a sales tactic. The idea of attaching glass balls of clear, colored or quilted glass became popular. The sales pitch was that a broken ball would tell the farmer that his barn would have been struck if the lightning rod hadn't saved it.

Sometimes a weather vane was attached to the rod and bore silhouettes of horses or cows, more often a rooster; the reason weather vanes also got named weathercocks. An advantage of the weather vane was alerting the farmer about times to take off from his chores to go fishing: "Wind from the east, fish bite least; wind from the west, fish bite best; wind in the south blows bait in the fish's mouth."

With the passing of years both weather vane and glass balls became the antique dealers sought-after prizes. The glass balls, translucent, mirrored or of opaque glass in a wide spectrum of colors, had metal capped holes at each end so they could be slipped onto a lightning rod and usually measured $3\,{}^1\!/_2$ to $4\,{}^1\!/_2$ inches in diameter.

Smooth tongued pitchmen, after clinching a deal with grim tales of lightning havoc, drew out sample kit ornaments from a velvet covered box to tempt the farmer's fancy. Besides balls the salesmen offered glass pendants to hang from the rod and metal embellishments as weather vanes to screw on top of decorations.

When antique collectors got involved and set their collectors' prices, they had three criteria for the balls: pattern, markings, and colors of glass. Some balls were smooth spheres of glass. Embossed balls had more value, often bearing swirls, pleats, ribs and quilt-like crosshatches. Shapes might resemble onions, doorknobs or chestnuts. The maker's name enhanced the value – James F. Goetz (JFG) of Wisconsin, was one of the best known.

Many balls bore a name: Electra, Hawkey, and Diddie Blitzen. The latter name came from the firm of self-styled Professor F. Diddie who added the German word for lightning to his name.

In the late 1930's some balls were made of glazed ceramic. After the 1940's plastic and pressed glass pieces, less decorated, appeared but didn't attract a collector's interest.

Those lightning rods atop my barn and house glistening above the land I know now are the envy of collectors who seek the blue and clear glass balls. However, the intentions of some so-called experts are subject to question.

Chapter XXIV

HEAVENLY THEATER

ny night is theater night if cloud curtains are sufficiently withdrawn. As a dweller on the highest hill of my Kettle Moraine acreage I have an unobstructed expansive sky dome filled with dramatic episodes right down to the tree silhouettes marking distant horizons. Summer seating is on plushy grass terraces lit up by firefly ushers. There's indoor seating in winter behind picture windows softly lit by night sky reflections on snow and ice.

As a starter, I search out the bright stars that circle the North Star – the Dipper. Primitive people called it a prowling bear. Algonquin Indians saw the bear in four stars forming the dipper's bowl, followed by three stars showing the hunters tracking the bear's footsteps. Because the North Star remains equal degrees from the horizon like the observer is from the equator, it's been the fixed mark used as a guide by woodsmen and sailors.

According to the Greeks, the Great Bear included not only the seven stars of the Dipper but also several not so brilliant. The four stars of the bowl constitute the flank and shoulders of the bear; the handle forms the tail and seven other stars sprawl down from the left bowl corner to form legs. Eight other on the right of the vessel outline the tip of the nose and front legs.

So that all bears might know when to prepare for cold weather, the Indian's Great Spirit put the big bear with a little one, half his size, close to the North Star which is the hole of their den. As these bears move around the North Star, half of the year they pass beneath it —sheltered in their dens makes it winter. The other half of the year they are above, out of their dens, making it summer.

Near by the Milky Way stretches across the sky from horizon to horizon. The River of Light, said the Japanese. The Scandinavians called it the Pathway to Valhalla, Asgards Bridge, traveled by the souls of heroes slain in battle. American Indians regarded it as a pathway to the Happy Hunting Ground, the Road of Souls – a trav-el-way to the Land of the Creator according to the Iroquois.

Touching this pathway are Cassiopeia, on the North Star's opposite side from the Dipper, and the Northern Cross, Cygnus. Orion lies to the right, followed by his great dog wading into the Milky Way and his little dog on the opposite bank. Others standing by are Vega, Altair, the Gemini, Cepheus the King, Perseus and Andromeda. Beautiful in summer, the Galaxy appears especially glori-ous in winter when frost has swept away the soft haze of autumn.

Orion, the most strikingly beautiful of all constellations, shows himself in the southwestern sky on winter nights. On his shoulders he carries a blazon sun, more than 250 times larger than our own. Diagonally across, to the right and down, Rigel marks his leg. Between these shine the three stars of the belt, and below is the blazing light of fiery Nebula on his knee.

Behind Orion follows Sirius, the Great Dog Star, the brightest and nearest in our northern sky. Following to the left of Orion is Procyon, the Little Dog, a bright star. On a cold winter's night when boards snap with frost, look up and watch Sirius – he may be barking sharply.

Pegasus, the winged horse of Bellerophon, seems to be flying on his back as he climbs into summer's eastern dark blue yonder. Three bright stars plus the brightest in Andromeda form a four-cornered figure. They light up his forward shoulder, the lower neck, back and lower rear. Beneath Pegasus, around the middle of August at 9:00 p.m., swims a circlet of stars, Pisces, the fish.

Doomed to travel eternally around the pole, Cassiopeia is watched over by her jealous husband, Cepheus. She was the beautiful vain Queen of Ethiopia, mother of Andromeda. Because she boasted so much about her own beauty as well as her daughters', the Sea Nymphs begged the Gods to punish her. Consequently, Andromeda became chained to a rock, left as a sacrifice to Cetus, the huge sea monster. But Perseus came to the rescue. Cassiopeia, transformed into a group of stars and doomed to travel, is seated on a throne in summer when beneath the pole star. A crudely printed W marks the spot. In winter she ascends the sky, is tipped over on her head, and forms an M. Cepheus remains dim and obscure, a pulsating variable star.

Perseus stands below Cassiopeia's chair where a line of stars connect with the Square of Pegasus. The fourth bright star from the Square is borne on Perseus' breast. To the right and slightly below on the head of Medusa, Algol dims and brightens once every three days. Brilliant meteoric showers tend to burst around Perseus near August 10th. Meanwhile, Andromeda since her rescue, reclines on her back, head at the Square.

In ancient times the sky provided the clock that told the seasons, the

Draco,
the Dragon

months and the hours of the night. Time continues to revolve around a center, the North Star, and the Little Dipper provides the hand or marker. Stars are ever on the move too. Unlike the sun, they do not rise in the east and set in the west. The farther from the North Star, the greater the circle a constellation travels. Most constellations swing through so great an arc that they are hidden beyond the horizon at certain seasons. Ancient peoples looked for reappearance to herald events that shaped their lifestyles.

For example, Capella, a brilliant star in Auriga the Charioteer constellation, rises in the northeastern horizon during late August. It is the Harvest Star – time to reap for winter's needs. Rising in the mid-March twilight when a spring haze softens the southwestern horizon, Spica lights up the Virgo constellation. Spica, the legendary ear of wheat held in the Virgin's hands, reminds farmers that planting time nears. Aquarius, the Water Carrier or Weatherman arises in the south during September, warning of equinoctial rains.

Northern lights fill me with awe every time I see them. The most spectacular heavenly display I've ever witnessed happened directly over my hilltop. It caught me by surprise on a bright September night as I started off on a walk. Suddenly great long fragile pastel banners dropped down from the sky, whirling, twisting and weaving patterns. At times I thought I could almost reach up to grasp the gauzy streamers. It was as if a giant Maypole had descended from the heavens and its many colored streamers danced configurations in the hands of unseen players. The air was still except for faint swishing and tinkling sounds each time curtains of green crossed the sky. Nothing I surveyed around me explained the sound. I wondered if a distant angel chorus provided sound effects. I felt as if I stood in a great cathedral, witnessing a holy performance. How long it lasted I shall never know, I had experienced eternity – time stood still.

Many times, before and since, I have watched Northern Lights but none have been comparable. Ancient people believed the Gods, battling across the heavens and lighting the sky with their great flashing swords caused the display. The Aurora Borealis has yielded many of its secrets to scientific investigations but only some great hand can orchestrate a spectacular of the unfathomable dimensions that I witnessed directly over my land, honoring it.

Like the poet, Sarah Teasdale, who wrote about the night she stood on a hill feeling the ecstasy of seeing the heavens ablaze with stars of many colors, I too felt honored to be a witness to so much majesty.

CHAPTER FOOTNOTES
Teasdale, Sarah **Collected Poems** *"Stars"*
(MacMillian Company, New York 1968)

Williamson, Julia **Stars Through Magic Casements**
(Appleton & Company 1930)

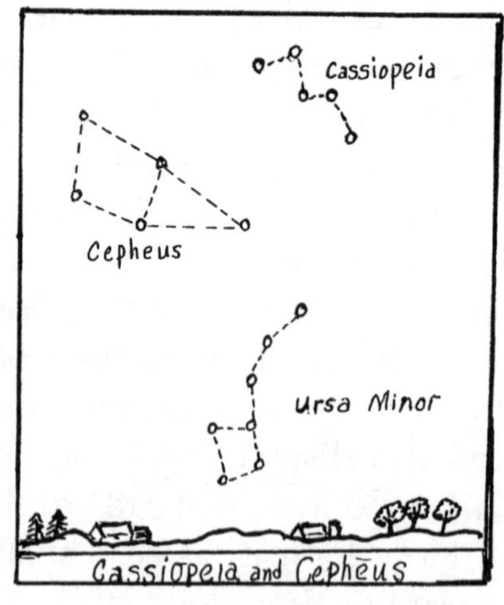

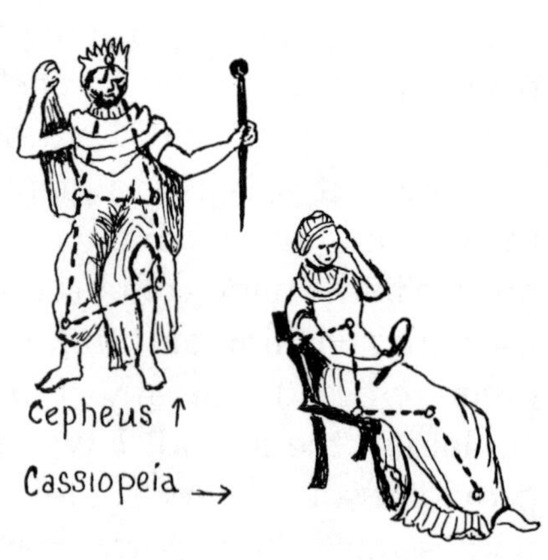

Chapter XXV

CAPRICIOUS MARCH

 dark sky on March 1, 1976, seemed just one of nature's moody spells. I had torn up January's calendar sheet and watched February's mixes of flurries, rain, sleet and fog wane and warm to some 40 degree days that invited strings of noisy honking geese weave across the sky. I sighed, glad that winter's back had been broken. How could I be so wrong!

By afternoon the sky turned black, bringing mixtures of freezing rain, snow, thunder and lightning. The next day dawned on a landscape totally captured in clear crystal. March aimed its worst backfire on Kettle Moraine country in 1976, breaking records in the state.

All of southeastern Wisconsin lay shrouded in so much ice that traffic, travelers, walkers, animals and anything that moved became immobilized. I watched a lone robin seeking a tree perch that didn't send him toppling into a nosedive. Intervals of thunder and lightning continued to rattle windows for two days. Then came the power outage.

By March 4th the storm abated, leaving in its wake several inches of thick ice coatings. Trees, branches, power lines, and poles crashed down under the heavy weight of ice. Tangled messes blocked roads and altered the landscape.

A phone call informed me that repair trucks could scarcely move. Damage was so extensive that repair supplies were very inadequate. Because the thick ice coating over the ground snow was so slick, loose objects and branches went careening wildly when touched by the slightest wind.

More freezing rain and strong wind came March 5th.

That night the top of the weeping willow tree south of the house crashed to the ground. Soon after that a loud crackling snap and thud vibrated throughout the house. The top half of the elm tree to the north had crashed, just missing the house. It threw a large branch across the top of my steep driveway.

That was as much as I could ascertain by flashlight.

March 6th, sunshine burst forth as if to appease the wrongs done. It was a crystalline, prismatic world, its sparkle too intense for the eye. However, the air was full of loud snapping and crackling, sounding like gunfire on a battlefield. Ice was cracking and branches were breaking, echoing and reechoing in the clear cold air.

Taking stock of my situation, it was obvious I was iced-in and would be for some time. My steep driveway was too slick for any vehicle to navigate the approximate two-block distance. The tree branches needed to be removed for the day a vehicle could attempt to climb.

I was without electricity to run the water pump, furnace, kitchen stove, freezer, lights, refrigerator, radio and clocks. That meant no water pumped for washing and toilets.

The family room fireplace, the only source of heat, needed to do duty also as the cook stove substitute. I had an 86-year-old ailing mother to be cared for. The only communication with the outside world, a telephone, functioned because its lines were mostly underground.

Thus began a daily routine. Chopping iced snow took precedence at intervals throughout the day. Loaded buckets were carried into the family room to melt. It took a bucket of ice snow 24 hours to melt down to a half bucket of ice water. That water was used for drinking, coffee, soup, tooth brushing and dishwashing.

Figuring out efficient ways to recycle water became a challenge. All used water went into a bucket that served to flush the toilet at day's end.

The family room fireplace provided warmth if one stayed within three or four feet of the fire. A large supply of firewood, stored on the enclosed porch beside the family room, required monitoring. It shrank all too fast since a fire needed to be kept burning day and night.

At night it meant I crawled out, at two-hour intervals, from the warmth of sleeping with my two dogs on the sofa bed, in order to add logs to the fire. My mother spent most of her days and nights wrapped in blankets in a reclining chair beside the fireplace. Temperatures in the rest of the house averaged around 37 degrees. The chance that radiator and water pipes would freeze was an ever-present concern.

Mealtime was an event.

An iron kettle suspended from a crane over the fire kept steaming water available. The best toasted bread and cheese sandwiches I've ever eaten browned on a wire stand over the coals. Potatoes wrapped in foil and tucked into the edges of the coals at breakfast were perfectly done by suppertime. I unpacked my camping utensils and was in business for cooking in style over an open fire. Supper began with the lighting of candles as daylight faded. A glass of wine celebrated the accomplishments of the day.

Besides chopping ice snow to fill buckets, my next priority was to remove the elm branches blocking the hill driveway. Since my hilltop terrain was a series of sloping areas and the glassy ice wouldn't permit me to remain upright, I had to figure out how to negotiate the 20 feet from door to elm branches. This was solved by knotting together lengths of clothesline, tying one end to a porch post and the other around my clothing-layered waist.

By sitting down it was an easy slide over to the branches with a saw grasped in my hand. Chipping ice layers from parts of branches to get at the wood tested my patience. As large sections of branches were sawed off, just the flick of a finger sent them sailing down the hill. Getting back to the house required pulling myself, hand over hand, on the rope.

My dogs, too, were unable to remain upright when going outside to relieve themselves. No matter what positions they tried, their hind legs would slide out, sending them sprawling. After the first shock and disbelief, they requested fewer outings and settled on locations at the edge of the front porch.

By March 8th the deep freezer was beginning to warm up, threatening to thaw the contents. So the next major project was to chop deep holes in the iced-over snowbank beside the porch. It took most of a day to do this and carry loaded baskets of frozen foods from the basement to the outside, then pack them into the holes. After these were covered over with more chopped ice, it was a matter of hoping that the warmth of the sun's rays wouldn't penetrate below.

Thanks to Alexander Bell, the telephone was a daily means of finding out what was going on elsewhere and bridging the sudden distance between civilization and isolated living.

One phone call came from Manitowoc, 20 miles to the northeast, where the effects of the ice storm were minimal. My report on the devastation and my survival predicaments, given as the reason I could not attend the County Highway Committee meeting as summoned was met with disbelief. At issue for me was losing the Committee's support on the Rustic Road system that I had been promoting and which was opposed by the Township Chairman.

Power lines, I learned, had to be entirely rebuilt from West Bend northward in a narrow band through the Kettle Moraine area. This had been hardest hit and we were at the end of the line. While other areas were returning to some semblance of normal functioning, the shortage of workmen, equipment and supplies would create delays for us.

March 12th, I heard electrical linemen on the road below my hill, sawing and chopping to clear the tangle of trees and wires. By mid-afternoon a loud noise on my steep driveway proved to be trucks wearing tire chains, slipping and slithering their way up as men shoveled sand in front of them. At the same time, some hard-hatted linesmen were creeping and chopping their way up the hillside through the woods to the electric light pole standing northeast of the house. They had to reattach the power line to the top of the pole.

The afternoon of March 13th, the long silence in the house was broken by what seemed the deafening but blessed humming of refrigerator and furnace kicking in – music to my ears.

And then there was light!

I turned on all light switches that evening and thanked Thomas Edison for his invention. A dinner feast to be prepared on the electric range depended on digging out food the next day from icy holes that substituted for the electric freezer.

March 15th, temperatures climbed to 60 degrees, remaining ice casings on trees and buildings were shed, and I returned to work. The first tub bath in two weeks felt like the height of luxury.

March wasn't finished with us yet. March 25th, thunder,

lightning, hail, rain and strong winds brought a twenty-four hour power outage. Funnel clouds the next day scared us with tornado warnings. The last day of the month rain and marble sized hail clobbered us. So began and so ended the month of March!

I welcomed Lady April with open arms! I think my land did too.

Chapter XXVI

ROADS - FOR WHOM?

 oads, mankind's pathways made wider by use, get one to where one wants to go. Historically they connected farm to farm, town to town, following the contour of the land. I took this for granted, choosing to live amid the picturesque peaceful hills and winding roads of the Kettle Moraine. Then one day my visions of the tranquil future were shattered by a newspaper announcement of a planned super highway to be built to cut a wide swath through these hills, obliterating vistas and disturbing nature's handiwork. A "time saver", they called it, connecting Milwaukee and Green Bay.

The "time saver" coming from Milwaukee would be one of three corridors. The preferred corridor would cut through some of the richest productive farmland, destroy some ancient forest land on its way to my Kettle lake, cut through my hill, usurping the site of my house and old timberframe barn, before continuing through my back woodland acres en route to Reedsville and Green Bay.

Bulldozers could rearrange the landscape but concerned citizens and we landowners were to be reckoned with first. The State Department of Transportation had waved a red flag and in January 1971 we were organized as the "Stop I-57 Environment Alliance." Our objectives were: (1) total opposition to an interstate highway in the area and (2) the improvement of highways that now served this area. We maintained that insufficient proof existed for need of another road since three state highways already served the region.

We expanded on issues at stake such as land loss to agriculture, wildlife habitats destroyed and shrunk, living space disrupted, unique glacial features (kames, eskers) and historical sites (Indian and family graveyards) disturbed, air and soil pollution, and more.

Our study of the highway design foretold problems. The design showed highway off-ramps only at major crossroads, dead-ending other rural cross roads. It divided many farm properties like a wall, barring access to adjacent land and preventing grazing animals, farm machinery and farmer activity from crossing over. The farmer's only alternative involved miles of driving to a major crossroad that would connect with roads accessing his disconnected acreage. Tunnels or overpasses were deemed too costly to be feasible. Roundabout routes also penalized time and mileage for emergency services such as ambulance, police and fire trucks. In addition people's homes were subject to relocation and nature's balance of natural features (watersheds and wetlands) would be disrupted.

Our Alliance efforts in acquainting the public with the implications of an Interstate Highway that would affect nearly everyone in the area began with local meetings in homes and progressed to public gatherings, forums and panel discussions. It attracted membership support from many organizations such as sportsmens' clubs, farmers' groups, womens' clubs and business groups. We involved our legislators and even consulted with the Governor. Local newspapers, radio and TV followed our actions continuously.

The end result after two years was the State Department of Transportation's decision to discontinue consideration of the preferred corridor, instead opting for the one paralleling the Lake Michigan shoreline to the east. They stated that this one better served the business traffic of more cities. It appeared that our Alliance represented the first citizen effort in history to sway a change in major highway construction plans.

Our Alliance next swung its support to the eastern corridor landowner concerns about routing the Interstate highway roadbed with regard to divided acreage, accessibility for land use and needs of emergency service vehicles. Some concessions were accomplished but not all landowners benefited.

Since our Alliance had researched the region for identification of features lying in the path of the proposed highway, subsequently relocated, the information about Manitowoc County held particular interest for our Manitowoc County membership. We felt the county information would lend itself to our development of a recreational brochure. We could evolve a map that linked together a route of secondary and lesser roads on which could be found such items of interest as photographic and scenic sites; historical places; glacial features; birding locations; unique wildflower and tree patches worthy of study and preservation; hiking, horse back riding and bicycling trails. One stretch of interesting roadway already used this way was the winding town road connecting Kiel and Cedar Lake, and bordering my acreage.

What a boon for the hobbyist this could be! It offered so much for retirees to enjoy without need to travel great distances. Working people and families short on time would have a nearby recreational resource. Slow paced travel speed could be mandated.

I presented the idea to the County Planner who agreed on the merits of such a brochure. He promised to sound out others and get back to me. He requested copies of our material, which I gave him.

Time elapsed without response. Then in 1973 newspaper publicity told that Earl Skagen, Department of Transportation, had reacted against billboards and streetlights marring the beauty of Wisconsin's rustic rural byways as well as some road developments. In 1974 he petitioned the State Legislature to designate a series of Wisconsin's scenic, lightly traveled rural roads for the enjoyment of motorist, bikers, hikers and nature lovers – to be called Rustic Roads.

Immediately I obtained an application and circulated petitions in the Township for approval to have some Township Roads submitted to the Rustic Road system. People seemed to favor it, particularly including the town road on which I lived. Not until I presented the application and petitions at the Town Board meeting did I learn that there were dissenters, namely Town Officials who had been considering widening and straightening the road on which I lived to improve traffic flow. Town residents attending the meeting voted in favor of the Rustic Road I had outlined but not the Town Officials.

The application process required the approval of the County Highway Committee. Their meeting was scheduled at the time in 1976 that I was iced-in and fenced-in by downed electrical wires due to a record-breaking ice storm that devastated the Kettle Moraine from Kiel to West Bend. I had no way of getting out of my iced hilltop and tangle of electric wires. Manitowoc City, the county headquarters, was bypassed by the storm so my predicament was incomprehensible as a reason for inability to attend the meeting. Ultimately the meeting was postponed but sentiment against a Rustic Road system developed and the idea was opposed at a later date.

Subsequent discussions with township residents indicated that the opposition received the support of business people who would lose money if roads weren't remodeled and believed a county goal should be the updating of all roads. The benefits from tourist and recreational dollars were viewed as minimal. Some objectors believed we lived in an age when speed and uncomplicated routes better served human needs. The issue a Rustic Road system highlights is whether there can be a co-existence of two differing objectives, allowing the preservation of old roads.

What is gained when highway speeds blur the views so that one arrives at his destination without having learned anything about the territory through which he passed? Do "time saver" roads accomplish anything toward reducing life's pressures when refreshment of body and soul seems so necessary for healthy survival?

I say, let no man tear asunder the adventure and peace that lurks on this Kettle land and its winding roads.

Chapter XXVII

WHERE DID YOU GO, MR. SCARE-CROW?

y wild Kettle Moraine hill acres are too wood-ed for a scare-crow to stand and catch the eye of road travelers and crows – but why is this stiff-bodied gent, sporting clothes that flap in the breezes, so hard to find on rural land else-where in my Township?

I remember when a ride in the country on a Sunday afternoon meant counting Burma Shave signs and scare-crows. I find no traces of Burma Shave rhymes now and scare-crows seem to have lost their jobs. Are they being dis-placed by burgeoning housing and shopping develop-ments or vast corporate farms that invade the clover and timothy fields and vegetable patches where the characters had presided? Or have they outlived their heyday and passed into the obscurity of past history?

There was a time when countrymen vied in bragging about whose scare-crow was the champion attention-getter. Undoubtedly their popularity suffered a blow when autos traded leisure travel for speedier runs. Traveling at sixty miles per hour or more doesn't allow the driver to take his eyes off the road and passengers have little time to study the fanciful scare-crows and award praise to the artful creators.

A scare-crow, according to Webster's dictionary, is "an object usually suggesting a human figure set up to scare crows." Protecting the planted land from seedling hungry crows prompted inventiveness in producing convincing guardian figures. Soon the farmer realized that competition with neighbors over the various guises of the figures also focused attention on whose plantings showed off to best advantage. The crows didn't care and were in awe of the figures till they got wise to the limited powers the gents possessed.

Scare-crows were supposed to look like major-domos of the territory but weather didn't always cooperate. They were outfitted in floppy jackets and pants that would swell out in the wind to resemble muscular heavyweight boxers. That changed on a windless day when muscular physiques became rather flabby. Rainy days brought out the worst of the body form – it looked downright limp and anemic, incapable of sending anything on the run. Sometimes even the head flopped to the side when rain soaked straw brains became waterlogged.

Perhaps those changes emboldened the crows to investigate. They tweaked the scare-crow's ear if he had one, pulled at innards that popped out as straw fibers and they walked the stiff arm's length. No retaliation.

Thereafter the crows could afford to become bolder. They took turns standing guard duty on the scare-crow's shoulder so that the other crows could scavenge the ground, dig up kernels and pull out green sprouts. The guard crow on duty sounded a screeching alarm if a real live man approached. They scattered before their presence was noted.

A top-flight scare-crow was always considered a work of art, I'm told. From late winter into spring whenever weather was unfit for man or beast to venture out, the artistic urge to produce the most remarkable scare-crow surged in the veins of the landsman. Like the high-water thaws of January that sent streams racing, the surge in the landsman sent him to his workshop in a cluttered barn or shed. There the rusty old iron wood stove was fueled and fired-up, the shop warmed to seventy or more degrees, and artistic and creative juices became free to flow.

An apprentice might have settled for a stake nailed on a crossbar but the master craftsman responded to the urge of genius. With a combination of holes and bolts, crafted arms and legs could transform the stake-bearing crosspiece into a suitable skeleton with right angles.

The crux of the creation was the face – either front or side view – made to look like a famous person or town character. Caricatures may be the joy of political cartoonists, but to actually produce a Teddy Roosevelt or the small town heckler in full form and dress was no mean accomplishment – it took some doing. To see the chap standing with arms stretched out, campaign style, would convince any passer-by of his importance as well as the perfection of planted rows under his surveillance. Add a threatening facial expression and crows would shy away.

The inspired landsman labored diligently bathed in stress perspiration, till his drawing on a wood slab achieved just the right exaggerated profile. In the process of sawing out a final silhouette the face might gain or lose a few characteristics but had to have a recognizable nose, chin, forehead, and Adam's apple. If that didn't work he could stuff a pillowcase and shape the face with stitches in strategic places and hope the problems weren't the same.

Not till the head got attached to the crosspiece stake, appendages fixed in place and the figure dressed for its destiny could it be called a work of art. Some vital decisions had yet to be made – whether or not to stuff the gent, paint his face with color and a smile, or outline features in black plus a frown, and select a hat style. When the completed gent was installed on his domain with some degree of ceremony and applause, he was on his own to deal with the crows. It was assumed that the crows would be properly intimidated and respectful of the gent's authority. If the scare-crow has now lost his job, how will future generations learn about this caretaker of the land's planted crops?

STIRRINGS OF
CHANGE

New House on same site

Chapter XXVIII

MY GOLDEN GIRL

he afternoon of March 4th warm sunshine melted snow into mud on the hilltop's north lower terrace, spring scented the air prematurely. Straw, covering a deep dug-up flowerbed that I intended to remodel in early spring with footings for a stone wall, kept that ground unfrozen. Instead I buried Trish here, saying my farewells as I looked down slope, across the frozen lake to the hills and ridges beyond. I remembered being told that the best place to bury a dog was in the heart. I had done so too, glad that mine was an elastic heart capable of stretching to encompass the fluctuating size dog family I had had and yet always make room for one more.

Adding one more became a comfortable habit. Need prompted Trish's adoption eight years earlier when the death of my aged ill mother created a gap to be filled. Sheba, my collie-German shepherd, had reigned supreme those eight years, making me feel unsure about her acceptance of a canine's youthful spirit invigorating our lives.

Trish was up against Sheba's strong-minded and assertive disposition. It gave me reason to feel apprehensive. I figured that the nonagressive, good natured, happy personality of a golden retriever female would be least threatening for Sheba. Trish at age 1 $^1/_2$ years had to leave the family that adopted her from the Humane Society, family illness and a pending move was the cause. She had coped with several cats, a feisty older dog, some foster children and middle aged parents. The day I visited her she won my heart. The day I took her away she was ready and eager to leave and never looked back – disconcerting for the family.

Trish's happy mood deflated, anxiety and fright made her reluctant to get out of my car when she encountered Sheba's hostile welcome and persistent loud barking. All my preparatory talk with Sheba counted for nothing. Sheba intended to intimidate and scare Trish so this intruder would leave her territory.

The first week Trish was miserable and homesick. Nothing was right with food, water or accommodations. I had to coax her to eat, cuddle and reassure her I wanted her. I found her to be an unusually sensitive, lovable little girl who hungered for affection which she promptly gave back in full measure. I discovered too that her eyes were quick to fill with tears if I was harsh or hurt her feelings.

Trish's accommodations for the first eight months or so were located on the enclosed porch off the family room where Sheba had her bed. A split Dutch door separated the two rooms. Curiosity could prompt either girl to stand on hind legs and peer over the half door. Since we were all under one roof, sounds and talk could be shared and hopefully feelings eased.

We made a noisy threesome in this process of working toward becoming a compatible family. I managed a powerfully loud voice to over-ride Sheba's loud objections and Trish's defensive yips. I had no intention of letting them fight the dominance issue and suffer ego damages. I made known my leader and boss role, with a hand to pet and cuddle each one, even at the same time.

My persistence succeeded. Sheba's objections diminished and the impulse to nip Trish subsided. I brought Trish into the family room a few times a day, keeping a watchful eye on actions. Eventually I coaxed them onto the sofa, one on each side of me. Tensions lessened. Soon they could share the room peacefully for longer periods of time.

However, outdoors was a different matter, I couldn't control actions there. Each went out separately. Happy-go-lucky Trish, a city girl accustomed to being walked on a leash, took off at a gallop each time as if she had the world by the tail. Freedom, space and discovering she had hunting dog instincts kept her occupied for hours. Checking every rabbit and animal scent to its source took her miles through the woods. Could she find her way back home? If she met a coyote would she flirt to win a playmate without realizing he was in search of a dinner?

I worried and walked the firelanes, whistling and calling, hoping she would orient to my sounds. One time I found her curled up exhausted, napping on the doorstep of a woodchuck's home on the rim ridge lane.

Sometimes she came home disguised. Her silky gold and white long hair lay plastered and matted with dried brown obnoxious smelling deer droppings she had rolled on. Her resistance to my scrubbing and grumblings didn't discourage repeats. Likewise, her efforts to rid the lawn of gophers brought on more scrubbings to de-earth her. She went after the creatures by digging their holes bigger and deeper till she disappeared from sight, seeming bent on digging her way to China.

The outdoors provided another entertainment, a smorgasbord of tidbits to be sampled. In season she helped herself to reachable raspberries in the patch, played ball with windfall apples and pears before munching them, tasted the assorted colored petunias in the flowerbeds, nibbled on chives and lovage in the herb bed, and anything else that caught her fancy. She was endowed with a stomach that could tolerate most everything.

Indoors I acquired a sidekick who stuck her nose into anything I put my head or hands into, mopped up all crumbs and spills on the kitchen floor with her tongue and claimed my favorite lounge chair that barely fit her. If I sat in it first she attempted to push me out. If that didn't work, she tried to sprawl on my lap. If I watched TV she did too, giving undivided attention to programs showing animals of zoo and jungle, cats, dogs and circuses. One program that fascinated her showed a man tossing balls to a dog. When she found neither one by sniffing around and behind the TV she went to the toy box, selected a ball, brought it to me and dropped it in my lap, looking at me expectantly.

Trish loved to play ball games. Sheba high-hatted all games. Eventually she couldn't resist muscling in to join the fun. Sheba didn't object to having Trish join our game of hide-and-seek. Both stayed-put till I whistled, then raced one another to find me. Sheba remembered some of my hiding places but Trish was quicker at scenting me out. Playing games together seemed to erase their frictions. They began taking naps within touching range of one another.

Trish's sympathetic nature blossomed as she recognized Sheba's arthritic whimpers when getting up or lying down and my sore movements following each of two hip replacement surgeries. She hovered close to us, careful never to bump. She nuzzled us, sometimes with teary eyes. No health problems for Trish so far.

I was in the midst of a series of chemotherapy treatments when I discovered lumps appearing on Trish's body. Rapidly developing lymphoma, the Vet said. Nothing could be done for her, not even chemo treatments. Both Trish and I were up against a cancer fight. My prognosis offered hope, hers didn't.

That such a lovable good girl could be dealt an immediate terminal future, deprived of a life she so enjoyed was unbearable for me. I lashed out at the unfairness in life's dealings.

Trish's deterioration moved phenomenally fast in a month's time. Appetite and energy faded, the once sparkling eyes plead for help and I was helpless. Her spirits drooped but she remained a loving and good-natured girl. She had no option. As we gazed into each other's eyes we knew it was time to say goodbye.

I held her frail body in my arms as the Vet eased her on to Doggie Heaven. Through my tear filled eyes I saw her look of resignation as our eyes met. I felt a sense of defeat – I had been unable to stop her ailment's progression.

I too was confronting unanticipated change with my own life. I wondered if some unseen power was steering our lives and toward solutions we were reluctant to make.

So goodbye Trish. You had the earmarks of a champion in my life. Your name may not glisten in record books or from a monument, but it does in my heart. The land will comfort you too.

Chapter XXIX

QUEEN SHEBA

ever had I been so thoroughly scrutinized. A large collie-German shepherd dog aimed an intimidating stare at me down a long arrogantly raised nose. We faced one another – Sheba stood inside a cage, I stood outside it at the Humane Society Shelter. Her stance made clear she was in charge of our encounter.

How could she know I was aching with longing for a dog pal and that my two pals had gone to Doggie Heaven a few months earlier. They had left me in an unbearably quiet and orderly house, no dog hair or spills as signs of life. I wanted a German shepherd-collie mix with guard dog instincts.

Sheba's demeanor clearly indicated that this was not the usual one-sided process of picking out a dog to adopt. Her attitudes were to be reckoned with – I just might not be acceptable to her. Sheba's size alone at age nine months was impressive, but so were the alert swiveling erect ears and velvety brown eyes. Besides, she was beautiful – long silky gold, white and black hair that swayed as she moved, reminding me of the collies who had raised me.

Sheba was recovering from an unhappy adoption experience, I was told. A young couple took her as a puppy to their small second floor apartment. They exerted rigid expectations for her behavior. Then a baby arrived. Space became crowded. Tensions evoked Sheba's defensive instincts. At age nine months they returned her to the Shelter, unmanageable they said. Sheba, disillusioned and frustrated, fought off any human handling. Shelter staff resorted to using long poles instead of hands. Though she had calmed down at the time I was notified of her availability she was still somewhat unpredictable.

I put our meeting to the test by asking to take her outside on a leash. The Shelter staff lined up to watch, prepared to rescue me. Sheba allowed me to attach the leash to her collar as I talked of the pal I wanted. She led the way to the door and outside. I knelt in the grass. She eyed me with a frown and stared, breathing in my face. I stared back. She moved toward me, pushed me over so I landed sitting down. Next she sat full weight on my lap and thoroughly licked my chin. I guess that's when we fell in love with one another for a lifetime of sixteen years.

She was nervous, a ticking time bomb, on the ride to her new home. The moment I opened the car door upon arrival she shot out like a sprung pellet, racing wildly around the hilltop, scarcely pausing long enough to check out smells. Then a car arrived unexpectedly, friends. Promptly Sheba stood beside me, barking furiously and displaying teeth. I introduced her to the word "friend" which she remembered thereafter meant an approved visitor. She had demonstrated the guard instinct I wanted.

Temporary lodging I told her would be in the workshop kennel apartment until she proved her plumbing system was under control and she didn't mess. She evidentially understood because two weeks later she proved her readiness for house living.

She also was quick to figure out that the novelty of exploring the wooded acreage held liabilities. She got lost. Burrs pinned her fur. Her high pitched shrieks for help became "I'm coming" yelps as she oriented to my calls and whistles. Burrs handicapped her movement. She lost patience with trying to chew them out and my slowness in untangling the masses. Thereafter she insisted that hikes with me stayed on cleared firelanes and balked against any detours that contained burrs and prickly bushes.

Shortly I realized Sheba did more to train me than my efforts did to train her. I learned to preface my requests with "lets do…" Bossing her invited stubborn resistance. Scoldings she saw as threat and attack, answering with growls. If my feelings were hurt she slobbered me with kisses. "No, nos" remained a touchy issue. She could tease, romp playfully, snuggle affectionately, and amuse with toys whose names she differentiated. There wasn't a mean streak in her but she could put on a threatening show, scare anybody.

Fortunately the Vet recognized her bluff too when she came to the Clinic. Her loud voiced tirade kept all at a distance but the Vet. Like a conquering hero she played her bluff. I coped with it seasonally when her allergy to grass pollens created an itch on her feet. By chewing the hair off her feet she tried to eliminate the itch, then licked the raw skin till it bled. My "no nos" and efforts to apply the Vet's ointment invoked growls and a showing of pearly white teeth. If she heard me approaching she tucked feet under herself and refused to show them. Blood spots and a guilty look told the story. I teased her about being funny and acting wild. Such remarks disarmed her, the tight lips melted into a wide grin. I then succeeded in applying the ointment when I promised to scratch her chest too. She'd roll over on her back for scratching and purr like a cat.

Sheba's comprehension of language and memory of vocabulary never ceased to amaze me. I first noticed it the day we were on a hike and I facetiously called her a pumpkin. She stopped dead in her tracks, eyed me with a disapproving growl and didn't resume her trot and wagging tail till I laughingly said I was teasing.

It was further evident in the way she remembered the voices of her favorites among my friends. Not only did she dote on them and offer frequent pawshakes when they visited, but she recognized voices on the telephone. Her favorite, friend Helen, moved from Kiel to Michigan but time lapses didn't fade recognition on annual visits or with the telephone voice. On long distance phone calls Sheba continued to paw at the receiver till I held it to her ear. I wished I could translate the sing-song noises she poured out to Helen. This probably accounts for her insistence that I use the phone daily or she would jiggle the receiver off its holder till I obliged.

Gradually I realized that I had a budding Phi Beta Kappa of Dogdom living under my roof. I think she viewed herself as a scant notch below me in peer status and could do most anything I did. She was a ready and quick learner – and I had to be too.

We had six years of getting to know one another when both my ill, aged mother, whom Sheba adored, and one of Sheba's special friends, died. Their deaths left a vacuum. I began talking about a sister for Sheba. We needed the revitalizing spirit of youth, I said. Despite serious apprehensions about Sheba's acceptance of a canine addition, I felt we could work through Sheba's likely strong-minded opposition to sharing home space and me.

I figured that the happy, unaggressive, good-natured disposition of a golden retriever female would be least threatening for Sheba. All my preparation of Sheba for Trish's arrival was for naught the day I introduced the eighteen-month-old youngster. Sheba felt no maternal instincts or curiosity, and voiced loud-mouthed vehement objections, hoping to scare Trish away.

I hoped the housing set-up would serve as a mediator, adjacent rooms. Sheba remained in the family room while Trish bedded down on the enclosed porch. A split Dutch door separated the rooms but allowed sounds and talking to be heard equally well. Either girl could rise up on rear legs and peek over the half door if prompted by curiosity about the other.

My determination to make the bonding work was up against Sheba's determination to eject the intruder. Repeatedly I had to out-voice Sheba's loud complaints and Trish's defensive vocal response. Sheba tried to nip Trish when I brought them together for brief intervals. I didn't allow any confrontations that would establish dominance and damage egos, stressing my role as boss. Bit by bit my determination won over Sheba's efforts. It took eight months before I could trust Sheba's intentions when they were together in the family room

Then the miracle began to happen. The girls took naps within touching distance of one another instead of on their beds. One day I noticed that Sheba laid a paw on Trish's leg.

During the next eight years Sheba's bouts with urinary infections and arthritic hips became increasingly trouble-some. At one point when I was recovering from two hip replacement surgeries we commiserated together, she accompanied my whines over sore movements with her own. Sympathetic Trish nuzzled us both.

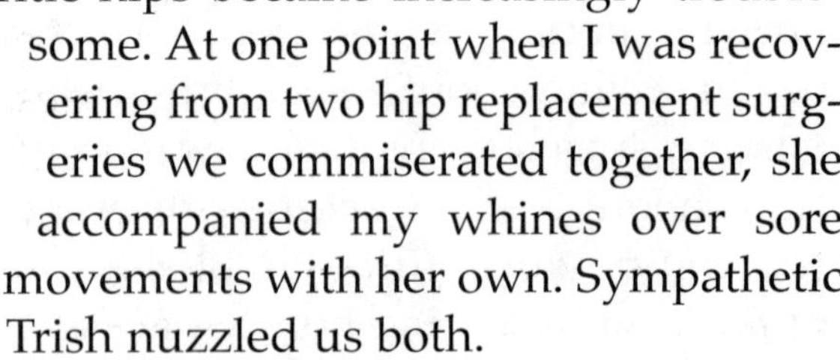

Despite her own discomforts at age fifteen Sheba became unusually solicitous of Trish who soon after began showing lumps on her body. A day that I came home from a chemotherapy treatment the Vet said eight-year-old Trish had rapidly growing lymphoma. Her condition deteriorated so drastically that she had to be helped to move on to Doggie Heaven. Sheba searched the house for her, coming to me with soft whines for an explanation. That was March and the earth was readying to renew life but for the three of us resilience no longer surged.

Sheba was in her sixteenth year, that same March — alert but eyesight slightly clouded, hearing less acute, and harassed by arthritis. Rear legs frequently collapsed, regaining an upright position sometimes failed. Without hip flexibility and strength I could do little to help her.

Winter conditions ahead loomed unmanageable for us both. If she collapsed on ice and snow she would be stranded without my ability to help.

My own health problems necessitated a painful decision – plans for the sale of my property and a move elsewhere. Sheba and I could carry on till winter's snows arrived, late October. Sheba would move on to Doggie Heaven and I to an apartment.

October 26, the day before my move, I sat on the family room floor cradling Sheba in my arms as we awaited the Vet's coming. Still in charge, Sheba's usual uncanny ability, to read my thoughts before they were spoken, told her that the time had come to say our good-byes. No tail wagging and throaty noises to express herself now. Instead her front paws clasped my arm and she pressed her warm body tight against mine, giving me the gift of her total self. My fingers lingered in her long silken hair as my tears washed her fur. She went to sleep with the composed dignity of the Queen she was. I thanked her for bettering me as a person and doubted that I had always measured up to her regard for me.

Queen Sheba

Though Sheba's body sleeps under the land's blanket on the hilltop's north slope, her spirit continues to claim me. I know because her long hair frequently works out of hiding places in my chair and sofa and clings to my clothes.

Chapter XXX

SNOOKIE

he Christmas of 1993 became Snookie's and my last one together in my home. As usual she smiled her pleasure from a little chair beside the five foot tall Christmas tree I had selected from my woodland and trimmed with ornaments from past family generations as well as those she and I had eyed together in my childhood.

Snookie came into my life the Christmas I was seven years old. We had moved to Missouri, hundreds of miles from my Wisconsin home where grandparents lived next door and Santa could find me.

Until Snookie came to me, nothing was right about the way Christmas Eve happened that year. Unlike past years, no big parlor doors opened slowly until they slid into the wall amid rising crescendos of "ohs" and "ahs" as a dazzling spectacle met our eyes.

In contrast, our Missouri tree was too small. Bright new ornaments didn't fascinate me like the 1890 variety that told stories of my mother's childhood. Light bulbs on the tree were no substitute for the twinkle and fragrance of bees-wax candles that magically lit up my grandmother's parlor. Even the presents under the tree reflected little of the thrill I had known.

It wasn't till I tore the paper off a large box, almost as tall as I, that a bit of the magic rekindled.

The box presented me with the most beautiful doll in all the world. Her dark eyes looked straight into mine, the dark lashes flickering coyly. Long dark curls of real hair framed a delicate pink happy face with rosy cheeks and dimples. A smiling open mouth, revealing two pearly white teeth, seemed to be whispering special words to me.

"Snookie!" I said over and over in an ever-louder voice. I was utterly enchanted. My grandfather's words of endearment long ago used this name with me, making me feel very special.

Snookie and I became pals from the start. She gave the companionship that I, as an only child, longed for. I introduced her as my "little sister" to any interested elders and to playmates. When train travel took me on visits to Wisconsin, I packed her outfits, styled like mine, in a little wicker suitcase. With Snookie modeling her garments we entertained train passengers en route.

Though Snookie wasn't my only doll, her status differed. My mother made attempts to teach me that, as the mother of dolls, it wasn't fair to favor one more than another. My emotions remained deaf to such ideas. She didn't understand that Snookie was my best pal and not one of "my children."

As the years rolled by my world expanded and other relationships took shape. Snookie was lovingly retired to rest in a box amid white tissue papers, on top of her neatly stacked apparel. She and the other dolls didn't see the light of day again till many decades later when, as a home owner, I emptied some boxes and trunks. I wanted to surround myself with treasures of the past.

The reunion with Snookie washed me in warmth as her dark eyes once more looked into mine, and her open mouth echoed words of years ago.

She and my doll family took over the bookcase and shelves on the walls of the second floor den. They gave the room a feeling of unstinting old relationships alive again.

They offered more comfort and support than the family portraits hanging on the walls of the hall stairway.

I could never bring myself to sell the dolls to collectors who thrilled over each one, especially those charmers who dated back to my mother's childhood. Two years ago a series of health circumstances brought the painful decision to a head. Snookie's future worried me most. She was the last to leave me.

An antique dealer I knew had a young daughter who adored dolls. The day I handed Snookie to her my old pal was dressed in a white coat over a blue checked gingham dress matching puffy bloomers underneath and lace edging on the white underslip. Her high-buttoned soft leather shoes and white socks showed off dimpled knees on ball jointed legs. Her ancestry was Armand Marseille 390 N.

Looking beautiful in all her twenty-six inches and smiling she accepted the transition though I felt tears clouding my eyes.

Six months later a phone call from the antique dealer excitedly relayed Snookie's latest adventure. Snookie had accompanied her to an antique show at a large new shopping mall. Seated on a chair in a booth she surveyed the hubbub.

During a lull in the foot traffic a teenager, her mother, and an older woman ambled along in conversation till they suddenly caught sight of Snookie. Lead by the older lady they came on a run to the booth shrieking, "That's her! That's exactly the way she looked! Even the dress and bloomers and shoes are the same!"

Carefully and affectionately they reached for Snookie, hugging and examining her, repeating their remarks.

"Forgive us for behaving like this," apologized the older woman to the antique dealer. "Never did we dream of seeing the doll Nana loved as a child and never forgot. She will have her ninetieth birthday next week. Her favorite doll was companion and confidant – understood her like no on else seems to these days, she says. Nana's mother sewed dresses with matching bloomers just like this. And her doll wore high-buttoned shoes. She was an Armond Marseille too,"

This doll would be the best birthday present for Nana that we could possibly get. She'd be thrilled!" eagerly suggested the mother to her two companions.

"But, Mother, Nana at ninety years is too old and maybe won't live long enough to enjoy the doll," commented the teenager.

"This doll will give Nana so much happiness she'll just have to live longer. Even if she doesn't, the happiness and pleasure of having her old buddy back again will give her peace of mind." Turning to the antique dealer the mother went on to say, "Nana loved that doll more than anything she had. One day when carrying her down the stairs Nana slipped and fell. The doll's head and body were too badly broken to repair. Nana never forgave herself and the hurt is still there."

"What will happen to the doll when Nana dies?" asked the teenager.

"She'll be mine," announced the older lady.

"And she'll be mine next, Sister, when your situation changes," said the mother, then turned to the teenager. "In time she'll be yours. Someday your children will love her too and you'll be able to tell them Nana's stories."

Snookie, smiling, was proudly carried off to her new home and heritage in Illinois. Tucked inside her is the long ago love of a little girl who grew up, and in later years made Snookie part of the Christmas spirit that glows from the trees given life by Windymare's Kettle Land.

Chapter XXXI

WINDS OF CHANGE

his Kettle land beckoned long ago and I never regretted agreeing to put my roots in its soil. Not only has it sustained me since but it has healed the bruising and physical wear and tear that living, aging and circumstance could impose. It gave me a joy of living, a status quo that I thought could go on forever – never thinking that the body's ability to carry on might falter. Harsh reality intruded and set the winds of change in motion.

To be summoned to a doctor's office on a Saturday morning when the office normally is closed sounded an ominous tone for me. Guests due for lunch that day would not excuse me. It didn't ease my mounting anxiety at the doctor's office to hear the nurse whisper to him, "Are you going to tell her today?"

Suspicions raced through my mind. I hadn't been able to overcome a series of colds. I couldn't shrug off waves of tiredness. My skin bore patches of black and blue spots that I couldn't account for. An inner voice that I tried to squelch hinted that my symptoms resembled those of my aunt who died the previous year of leukemia.

The doctor wasted no words. Test results following my annual physical exam pointed to leukemia. It was November 1979. More definitive tests were scheduled immediately at a Milwaukee Hospital. A week there and the diagnosis was chronic lymphocytic leukemia. I was told to get my affairs in order. The leukemia tended to become acute in five years, then terminal. Hearing this unnerved me. I saw my future disintegrate. I felt powerless, angry, overwhelmed, and frustrated but not ready to concede a future and plans for retirement years. I had to fight the leukemia, I told myself, and devise ways to defeat its inroads. I would adapt to the swing of life but not let the leukemia direct it.

Something happened. I developed a new acute sense of my being – colors, sights, sounds and even insignificant happenings all took on a richer depth. Life could no longer be taken for granted. Time held an essence to be savored.

I resumed my habit of taking long walks on my land but with the added sensuality of feeling the soil underfoot and the texture of growing things. The earth seemed to reach out and envelop me; earth and grass exhaled pungent perfumes like never before and when I sat in the damp grass the moist greenery felt like soothing ointment on hot skin. The smells clung to my clothing as if reluctant to let go. My doctor grandfather's words flashed in my mind, "Windymare with its unpolluted air, pure water and uncontaminated soil will heal and keep you well, its peacefulness will soothe your worries. Hang onto it. Care for it and it will care for you."

I credit the land with helping me keep the leukemia under a measure of control in the years that followed but arthritis in twelve years handicapped me so painfully that two total hip replacements became necessary. Since steel hips lack the flexibility of normal leg structure, walking woodland trails proved hazardous and uneven ground required the support of a cane. Daily walks with my dogs were marked by rest stops on grassy slopes with seating humps. Here we could absorb the land's resiliency and fragrances. I felt refreshed. The land not only had a healing touch but also erased awareness of corporal limitations and called my attention to its thriving smallest population.

A succession of physical problems during the winter of 1994 built into a painful decision I hadn't anticipated. Trouble began with what I thought was a severe sinus cold, diagnosed after I lost the sight of my left eye – Temporal Arteritis, a rare condition of inflammation of blood vessels in the head. Efforts to save my eyesight and a leukemia flare-up necessitated chemotherapy treatments. It was winter, the heart of the snow and ice season. My isolated hilltop presented unwelcome icy challenges to drivers needed to transport me weekly or oftener to medical resources in Sheboygan.

I knew in my heart that my kinship with the land had its limitations. While I was still able to carry out plans this was the time to take action for the sale of Windymare and move on to easier living. Reinforcement came from frustrations with eyesight problems, associated with the permanent sight loss in one eye, and spells of losing consciousness that were later diagnosed as cardiac arrhythmia. A vigorous lifestyle of activities and interests could no longer be handled by my physical body, a realization that verged on tearing me apart.

As spring blossomed I sought comfort in the feel and smell of earth and grass, taking my sadness to the land and talking out the pros and cons of the decisions that lay ahead. I mixed my tears with the dewy freshness of growing things and felt their blessing.

The chance that this land might get into profiteering hands rather than those of the preservationist alarmed me. To that end I renewed my Forest Crop and Woodland Tax acreage contracts with the State Department of

Natural Resources for a fifty-year period. Hopefully this served as protection against slicing the land into sale lots and lumbering woodland. Among potential buyers few shared my preservation interests and practices.

During the summer of 1994 a couple with seemingly similar interests as mine and with the intent of making this their lifetime home negotiated the purchase of Windymare's 120 acres. As legal papers and signatures proceeded, including the legally required series of evaluations and so-called improvements for sales purposes, I was shaken over knowing I had passed the point of no return. Could I sustain my belief in the decision I had made? Could I trust that I had put the land in good responsible hands? Would they live up to their promises to preserve, protect and hold together the 120 acres?

Next came the dismantling of a home that harbored inherited possessions of several generations plus my own accumulations, all abounding in memories. In the next six months antique dealers I knew and friends carried away my treasures. I had to downsize my possessions to fit into a two-bedroom apartment.

The process, like a long reeled film, took me through a review of my life, even reviving forgotten and faded events. Such things as scrap books, old letters and photos way-laid my progress. I fought their disposal in the trash barrel fire, dictated by lack of future apartment space and unlikely usefulness. In the burning I watched my life disappear and move out of reach in the rising smoke. What if memory couldn't hold onto the details without these props? If memory failed me what would I have left of a vital life to hang onto?

October 27th marked the day the movers left me with an empty house – a shell holding the echoes of memories. I walked around the rooms thanking the house for what we shared, joys and sorrows blended and mellowed into a good life. As if to honor the past, the warm October setting sun entered uncurtained windows and gilded the rooms.

Next I walked alone around my hilltop, breathing in deeply the scent of fall leaves crushed under my footsteps and I imagined the woodsmoke smell that customarily drifted down from the fireplace chimney at this time of year. Only the chickadee's lively prattle penetrated air stilled by the departure of birds for the southland.

I sat on a limestone step on the north slope's terrace long enough to say goodbye to my dog pals buried there. We had shared the same joys of this land and believed our lives would carry on forever. Yet one day our bodies faltered and change became inevitable. We had often sat together on this spot, overlooking the tree-rimmed lake below and the rolling hills beyond. They stretch to a wooded ridge where a white steepled church snuggles in a hollow. I watched the blue sky above melt into the reds, golds, pinks and lavenders shot out by the setting sun. The sunset promised a good tomorrow.

Though change takes me away from Windymare, its land has worked a hold on me and I will stay in touch, mainly by writing about my life and adventures there.

AFTERWORD

nable to foresee how the future would evolve, it was fortunate I didn't know the troubling twist that lay ahead. In three years the buyers reversed themselves on promises made to me and put Windymare up for sale. They sliced the land into parcels for profit sales, maneuvered the land contracts to make it possible. The husband had lost his job and felt the solution to be a move elsewhere.

The place was unoccupied for a winter til a local area couple saw and fell in love with it. They purchased the thirty one acre parcel surrounding the house and hoped to eventually purchase most of the other parcels as yet undisturbed by real estate development. Windymare will keep its name. It is my hope that their interest in preserving and protecting Windymare can one day make it whole again.

That Windymare's land has endowed me with its healing touch, despite disruptions of my physical functioning, is evident in the continued zest for living that shapes my days. Twenty years have passed since my leukemia diagnosis predicted a time limited statistic. In turning to writing these episodes I have felt the land's energy surge through me, bringing joy in discovery of unrealized strengths. I had given up pursuit of my art hobbies when I lost sight in one eye. I rose to a friend's challenge that I do pen and ink sketches for this book – a self retraining of hand and eye coordination I hadn't thought possible. Writing and sketching for this book has been a labor of love and appreciation for the way Windymare's land has sustained me.

APPENDICES

Recipe Shelf Recipes
Chapter Reading Suggestions
Acknowledgements
Notes ----

A few recipes I relied on to take me through the seasons and to serve visitors. Frequent usage made them a tradition at Windymare on Kettle Moraine land.

For the BIRDS...

Mix Mash

1/2 Jar of creamy peanut butter

Fats saved from cooking *(bacon grease)*; fats cut off meats; fine cut meat scraps...melt together.

Add: 2 to 4 cups yellow corn meal (enough to make wobbly paste, but not stiff) and stale nut meats, bread crumbs, if on hand.

While hot: stir together and mix well. Let stand till cool and stiffens. Spoon into bottom of plastic bottle cut as a holder.

Mash Holder

To make a Mash Holder:
Wash bottle well, cut so bottom half has side tabs for hanging. Punch holes in each tab. Attach heavy wire to hang. Mash will harden in cold temperature. Birds love it!

Dog Hair Holder

For lining nests with dog hair and yarn remnants, any color (red preferred), hang against tree trunk.

To make Holder: Use wood for sides, bottom, back and top. Size: about 8" by 8", 3" deep. Drill 2 or 3 holes in bottom for air vents. Attach lid top with hinges for raising to insert hair. Wire grill allows 1" square spaces for birds to hang on while grabbing hair and yarn.

Favorite DOG SNACKS...

Canine Treat Biscuits

1 carrot
2 ½ cup flour
1 egg beaten
½ cup powdered milk
⅓ cup cold water
1 teaspoon brown sugar
1 teaspoon salt *(optional)*
⅓ cup melted shortening

Grate carrot. Add: powdered milk, egg, water, sugar and shortening. Mix well, shift in flour (unbleached) Dough will be stiff. Roll out to ¼ or ½ inch thickness Cut with cookie cutter or in stripes, place on lightly greased cookie sheet. Bake 25-30 minutes at 350. Cool on rack.

Corn-Wheat Canine Treat

2 cups whole wheat flour
½ cup corn meal
1 egg beaten
1 teaspoon salt *(optional)*
1 teaspoon brown sugar
½ cup white flour
1 apple grated
½ cup melted shortening
⅔ cup water

Mix all ingredients together, mix well.
Roll out to ¼ inch thickness.
Cut out with cookie cutter.
Bake 35-40 minutes at 350°

Spice Cookie
(favorite of Prince & Blackie)

1 cup butter, plus ¾ to 1 cup sugar. Cream well. Add to: 2 eggs well beaten. Add ½ cup sorgum or molasses. Beat total. Add 4½ cups sifted flour to which was added:

3 teaspoons ginger
1 teaspoon soda
½ teaspoon salt
½ teaspoon cinnamon
½ teaspoon nutmeg
½ teaspoon cream of tartar

Sift together several times. Add 1 tsp. ground anise or a few drops of liquid anise. Mix well, shape into 2 rolls, chill overnight, slice and bake, 350° or 375°
(If dough was packed in wax paper lined pan, it's easier to cut lengthwise or in strips)

HERB BED and SPICE MIXES...

Fine Herbs Mix

2 tablespoons savory
2 tablespoons dried
    parsley
2 tablespoons thyme
2 tablespoons grated
    lemon rind
2 tablespoons sweet
    marjoram

¹/₂ tablespoon sage
1 tablespoon celery seed
    powdered
1 teaspoon bay leaf
    powdered

Mix and store in a shaker. Improves: roasts, stews, soups, steaks or any meat dish.

Herb Salt

2 tablespoons thyme
2 tablespoons bay leaf
2 tablespoons pepper
1 tablespoon cloves

1 tablespoon
nutmeg
1 tablespoon marjoram

Mix, press through fine sieve. Add 4 tablespoons fine salt. Store in tight jar. Improves: meat, poultry, fish.

Spice Mix

1 tablespoon nutmeg
1 tablespoon cinnamon

1 tablespoon cloves
1 tablespoon sugar

Use in all types of cooking. Store in tight jar.

No-Salt Herb Blend

4 tablespoons
    oregano leaves
4 tablespoons onion powder
4 teaspoons marjoram
    leaves
4 teaspoons basil leaves
4 teaspoons ground savory

4 teaspoons garlic powder
2 teaspoons thyme leaves
2 teaspoons rosemary
    leaves
1 teaspoon sage leaves
1 teaspoon ground black
    pepper.

Combine above in bowl. Crush small amount at a time *(use mortar and pestle or back of spoon)*. Store in shaker or tightly covered jar. Use over fish, chicken, salads, vegetables, etc...Yields 1 cup.

Salad Seasoning

4¹/₂ tablespoons onion powder
2 tablespoons poppy seed
1¹/₂ tablespoons garlic powder
¹/₃ cup toasted sesame seed *(toast in skillet, cook & stir over med. heat til golden, 2-5 min.)*

1¹/₂ tablespoons paprika
³/₄ teaspoon celery seed
¹/₄ teaspoon ground black pepper

Combine all, spoon into shaker or tightly closed jar. Sprinkle over greens, sliced tomato, cold vegetables, cottage cheese or use in salad dressings. Yield: 1 cup

Seeded Salad Dressing

³/₄ cup vegetable oil
2 teaspoons Salad Seasoning from above

¹/₄ cup cider vinegar

Combine. Shake well. Serve over: mixed greens, cold vegetables, sliced tomatoes, etc...Yield: 1 cup

Quickie Low Sodium Seasoning:

Mix thyme and garlic

Morel Mushrooms in Springtime

Usually appear around Memorial Day in moist shaded soil, grow 2-6 inches tall, top resemble a sponge. Not easily confused with toxic mushrooms, bears little resemblance to other kinds...Cut stem at soil level, wash well, don't soak. Cut into bite size pieces. Saute in butter till a deep golden tan, stir often. To serve as a snack use toothpicks to spear...Can be served with meats on a dinner plate. If only partially sauted can be frozen and further sauted at a later date.

Puffball Mushroom in Fall

Round or oval, can reach size of a football. Use only in pure white stage. Resembles no toxic mushrooms...Wash and peel off thick white skin. Cut flesh in strips, $1/4$ or 1 inch wide. Saute in $1/2$ butter and $1/2$ olive oil for about 4 minutes at medium heat till each side is golden brown, not dark. Sprinkle with chervil, nutmeg, salt and pepper, lightly...Can be served as a snack or in place of meat. Makes large quantity. Freezing for storage is not recommended.

Puff ball

Raspberry Cordial

Fill quart jars $3/4$ with raspberries (unwashed) and imperfect. Boil together $1\frac{1}{2}$ cups sugar and $1/2$ cup water. Pour over berries. Sprinkle $1/2$ cup sugar on top each jar. Fill jars with Brandy. Screw lid on tightly. Store in brown paper bag til Christmas. Drain jar to serve. Enjoy strong raspberry fragrance.

Keep berries in same jar. Add Rhine wine or Muscatel. Let stand in brown paper bag til Easter. Serve.

Berries, either time, are delicious served over ice cream.

Raspberry Preserve

4 quarts raspberries   9 cups sugar

Wash berries, sprinkle with sugar. Let stand 12 hours. Cook about 10 minutes. Pack in clear glasses and let stand in sunshine for 2 days. Yield: 4 half-pint jars

RASPBERRY SEASON Specialties...

Shortcake
(Raspberry Topping)

Grease 9 inch cake pan with 1 tablespoon butter Combine: 2 cups flour sifted, ¹/₄ cup sugar, 4 teaspoons baking powder sifted, ¹/₄ teaspoon salt, dash of nutmeg and sift total into bowl...Cut ¹/₂ cup butter into this to resemble coarse meal. Blend in measuring cup: ¹/₂ cup milk, 2 egg yolks using fork. Stir into flour mix, make soft dough. Next pat out in prepared pan (dust fingers in flour lightly). Brush surface generously with egg whites and sprinkle with 3-4 tablespoons sugar. Bake in preheated 450° oven, 12 minutes or til golden brown. Cool on rack

Ice Cream
(with Raspberries)

Separate 5 eggs *(save whites for Farina Pudding)*. Put yokes in double boiler. Add: 1 cup sugar, 1 carton ¹/₂ & ¹/₂ cream, ¹/₄ teaspoon salt...Cook til thickens, remove from heat. Cool a ¹/₂ hour.

When cool add 1 overflowing tablespoon vanilla.

Pour into ice cube trays to freeze til hard. Remove, cut up ice cream, put in electric mixer. Beat til ice cream rises to near top of bowl.

Store in plastic cartons and freeze. Ready to use.

Farina Pudding

Use egg whites left over from ice cream.

In double boiler put: ²/₃ cup Cream of Wheat, 3¹/₂ cups water or milk, ²/₃ cup sugar, and when thick add 1 tablespoon vanilla.

To whites of 5-6 eggs *(1 cup=8 small eggs)* add pinch of salt and beat til stiff.

Fold in cooled Cream of Wheat mixture. Cool a few hours.

Serve with chilled fruit topping, raspberries preferred.

Raspberry Herb Tea

¹/₂ cup dried red raspberry
   leaves
¹/₂ cup crushed mint *(any
   variety leaves from
   herb bed)*

1 teaspoon nutmeg
1 teaspoon cracked cloves
1 teaspoon dried orange
   or lemon peel

Put in gallon glass jar. Fill with water and place in sun for several hours.

Sweeten with honey according to taste.

Damson Plum Jam & Sauce

ORCHARD Delights...

I was introduced to Damsen plums as dessert at Williamsburg Inn, Williamsburg, Virginia, and saw them growing on small trees in the gardens. I wanted a tree and learned that these trees were adaptable to the Wisconsin and Kettle Moraine climate. The small deep blue plums made my tree a vision of blue in the fall. I never sprayed it. The tree didn't seem insect prone.

Sauce: to be canned, eaten plain or over pudding & ice cream. Boil into syrup: 1 cup sugar & 2 cups water. Pour over plums (pits removed) and packed into jar...Seal...Give a 20 min. hot water bath or prepare by open kettle method.

Jam: Cook plums in as little water as possible. Press through a collander to obtain pulp. Boil: 1 cup water, 1 cup pulp, ³/₄ to 1 cup sugar. Stir often. When drip from spoon becomes stringy and stops, fill jars. Seal.

Apples for Apfel-Brei

A generational family favorite dating before 1857, brought from Germany.

Proportions listed can be doubled or tripled:
3 pounds apples, peeled and cored, cooked in almost no water til soft, sugar added to taste.

In another pot cook 1 pound white potatoes, peeled, til soft. Drain and season with salt.

Mash...mix apples and potatoes, heat well and serve in large bowl with enough browned butter to cover top generously.

We always used the same Ironstone bowl for serving. Meat served with it might be hamburger patties, pork sausage or pork chops.

Apples for Apfel-Kuchen

An equally old generational family favorite brought from Germany.
Yield: 12 servings *(fills 2 regular size coffee cake tins)*. Cream together: 2 tablespoons shortening and 2 tablespoons sugar...In a cup beat 1 egg, fill cup with milk and add. Next add 2 cups and 2 teaspoons baking powder. Stir well...Divide batter into 2 greased tins. Use spoon to spread dough evenly up sides of tins. Place peeled quartered apples generously on top. Make Streusel: 2/4 cup white sugar, 3/4 cup brown sugar, 1/2 cup flour, 4 tablespoons butter...Mix and crumble with a little cinnamon and nutmeg. Spread over apples. Bake 350°

Concord Grapes for Juice

Strip grapes from clusters, wash. Cook in large pot with a minimum of water.

Mash through strainer. Do not add sugar, usually sweet enough.

Store and freeze in plastic cartons.

When serving add water only to extent thinning is needed.

Pear Honey
(for toast & muffins

6 pears
2 apples
1 orange and rind

1/2 lemon
1 1/2 pounds sugar

Grated orange rind, peel off white inner skin to discard. Pare apples and pears. Discard orange seeds and cores. Combine orange, apples, pears and peeled lemon. Grind together.

Add sugar and cook 20 minutes, adding grated orange rind.

Cook until thick. Put in jars and seal.

Pandel's Famous German Pancake

Pandel's Whitefish Bay Inn, Milwaukee's long time restaurant, serves this memorable pancake; recipe published in the Sheboygan Press 5/14/69. Recipe makes large pancake, 2 large servings or more if you cut into smaller portions.

1/2 cup all purpose flour
1/2 cup milk
1 tablespoon butter
1 tablespoon shortening
4 large eggs
Pinch of salt

Mix flour, milk, salt together til smooth. Crack in eggs and mix til smooth. Melt butter and shortening in large frying pan *(preferrably with sloping sides)* and add mixed batter. Fry til golden brown, then turn with spatula. Make 4 criss-cross cuts *(2 each way)* with spatula. Bake at 425° for about 12 min. in oven. Pancake will not begin to rise til about 7-8 min. Serve immediately. Serve with maple syrup, powdered sugar, jelly, bacon or any other accompaniment preferred.

"Oh Boy" Waffles

2½ cups flour
¾ teaspoon salt
4 teaspoons baking powder *(calumet preferred)*
2 eggs
2½ cups milk
1½ tablespoons sugar
¾ cup melted shortening or salad oil

Sift dry ingredients. Combine eggs, milk and shortening. Combine liquid and dry ingredients just before baking and beat til smooth. Batter is thin. Bake in hot waffle iron. Yields: 10
Serve with warm Honey Butter Sauce: 1 cup liquid honey in double boiler, add ¼ cup butter, ¼ teaspoon cinnamon, dash of nutmeg, and mix together.

Lentil Soup

Quantity fills several freezer containers. Soak 2 bags lentils overnight. Drain and use water to cover ham skimpily. Simmer *1 hour (large piece of ham with bone)*
Add: lentils, 1 onion cut fine, pepper, garlic powder, add any left over lentil water or other as contents need thinning.
Simmer 2½ hours. Cut up ham. Quantity may require dividing ham and lentils between 2 cook pots to accomodate next additions.
Add: stewed fruit *(1 pkg. mixed dried fruit and 1 pkg. prunes stewed together)*. Divide between two pots...Add to each pot: 1 scant tbsp. sugar, ¼ tsp salt, and a little lemon juice to suit taste. Simmer briefly. Cool, store in freezer.

WINTER Warm Ups.. Freezer ready.

Lazy Daisy Bean Soup

Soak 2 cups Great Northern Beans overnight...Drain. Cover 2-3 smoked ham hocks or large ham hunk with bone with 2 quarts water. Simmer 2½-3 hours. Remove meat and cut in pieces, eliminating fat. Then return meat to its broth after fat was skimmed off top of cooled broth. Heat and add: 1 large onion cut up, 1 large can tomatoes, several garlic clove cut up, 1 large red pepper or 1 teaspoon chili powder, juice of 1 lemon (optional), salt and pepper to taste. I added a little Spike seasoning too..Let cool. Time improves flavor.
Stores in freezer a long time.

Cheese Strips

Serve Cheese Strips with Soup:

Butter both sides of bread slices, cut in strips and cover with cheddar cheese slices.
Sprinkle paprika on cheese, Lay on cookie sheet.
Toast under broiler til cheese melts.
Serve warm.

Snow Pudding

1 pint boiling water
1 cup sugar
3 egg whites

2 tablespoons cornstarch *over juice and rind of* 1 lemon (*grated*)

Boil water, cornstarch, lemon and sugar til thick and done. Gradually pour this into stiffly beaten egg whites, stir til well mixed. Chill in refrigerator several hours.

Custard Sauce: in double boiler cook yolks of 2 or 3 eggs with 2 tablespoons sugar, pinch of salt, 1½ cups sweet milk.

Cook til thick but runny. Flavor with vanilla. Serve cooled over Snow Pudding (*a generational family recipe*)

COFFEE or TEA TIME with Visitors...

Sour Cream Coffee Cake

Originated and served by rug hooking groups at break time. Cream together till thouroughly mixed: ¾ cup margarine or butter (room temperature) and 1½ cups sugar...Beat in: 2 eggs till mixture is light and fluffy...fold in: 1 cup sour cream and ½ teaspoon vanilla...Then sift together and fold into mixture 2 cups flour and 1 teaspoon baking powder. Spoon half of mixture into greased floured angel food cake pan. Sprinkle half of topping over batter. Spoon remaining batter into pan and spread evenly. Sprinkle remaining topping on top. Bake 350° for 45-55 minutes *(till wooden toothpick comes out clean).*

Topping: mix together ½ cup chopped walnuts, 2 tablespoons brown sugar, 1 teaspoon cocoa, 1 teaspoon powdered sugar and ½ teaspoon cinnamon.

Menu

Snacks to serve with wine or other drink

No-Peak Casserole - Serve over rice

Uncle Ben's Long Grain and Wild Rice with herbs and seasonings.

Bran Muffins *(fresh baked or frozen or heated)*

Fruit Gelatin Salad

Frozen cooked vegetable *(whatever is on hand)*

Dessert: Ice cream pie *(freezer supply)*

Snack

Unsalted oyster crackers, 1 pound bag

Mix together heaping ½ teaspoon: dill weed, lemon pepper, garlic powder and ½ cup olive oil. Put crackers in a big cake pan, pour mixture over them, stir frequently while they stand several hours til oil is absorbed and ingredients adhere. Do not heat.

Put in jars.

Will keep indefinitely in refrigertaor.

No-Peek Casserole

Can be prepared a day or two in advance, stored, covered in refrigerator. 2 pounds stew meat cut in bite size pieces. Put in greased casserole:

1 can cream of mushroom soup

1 can mushrooms drained or 1 pound fresh

1 envelope Lipton Onion Soup Mix

$^1/_2$ to $^3/_4$ cup burgandy or red wine

Stir in meat, cover and bake 325° for 2 hours. Do not peek til done. Serve over rice...Freezes well, keeps tasty with lengthy freezing time.

Bran Muffins

2 tablespoons shortening

$^1/_4$ cup sugar

$^3/_4$ cup milk

1 cup All-Bran

$^1/_2$ teaspoon salt

2$^1/_2$ tsp baking powder

1 egg

1 cup flour *(unbleached)*

Combine shortening and sugar, mix thoroughly, add egg and beat til creamy. Add All-Bran and milk, let soak til most of moisture is absorbed...Sift flour with salt and baking powder and add to first mixture, stir only til flour disappears. fill greased muffin pans or paper muffin cups $^2/_3$ full. Bake in moderate oven at 400° about 30 minutes. Yield: 8 large (3 in.) or 12 small (2$^1/_4$ in.) muffins

Bran Muffins
continued

Note: if sour milk or buttermilk is used instead of sweet milk reduce baking powder to 1 teaspoon plus $^1/_2$ teaspoon baking soda.

Variations: Bacon - add $^1/_4$ cup, crisp or dried, to dry ingredients

Nut - add $^1/_2$ cup chopped nut meats to dry ingredients

Orange - add 2 tablespoons grated rind to dry ingredients

Raisin - add $^1/_2$ cup to dry ingredients

Spiced - add 1 tablespoon molasses to creamed mix and $^1/_2$ teaspoon ginger or 1 teaspoon cinnamon to dry ingredients

DINNER GUEST Menu...

Fruit Gelatin Salad

In a pyrex bread or meatloaf pan (5¹/₄ in. W; 10¹/₂ in. L; 3 in. H.) cut up a variety of fruit in season (orange, melon, raspberries, plums, apples, grapes, pears, grapefruits, cherries) and pack pan ³/₄ full...Dilute 3 cans frozen orange juice with 3 cans water and from this measure 3¹/₄ cup into a bowl. Pour another ¹/₂ cup into a cookpot and add 2 packets of plain gelatin, stirring over heat til well dissolved. Mix with other liquid while hot, pour over the cut fruit. The pyrex pan will be filled to the top. Put in refrigerator to chill several hours. To serve I set pan in basket. The fruit gelatin needs no sweetening unless you like sweetened dressing. It keeps well in refrigerator several days under Saran Wrap cover.

Ice Cream Pie

Mix and melt together in double boiler: ¹/₄ cup butter and 1¹/₂ cups chunky peanut butter.

Combine 2 tablespoons sugar and 1¹/₂ cups graham cracker crumbs, melted butter and peanut butter, stir together and pat into a pan to make a crust, including sides.

Fill pie crust with 1¹/₂ quarts soft ice cream. Store in freezer.

Remove 15 minutes before serving to allow softening for cutting. Can be served plain or with chocolate, caramel or rum sauce.

Autumn Jell
My Favorite (Chapter XIV)

6 medium cooking apples
(preferably grown in the wild)
2 pounds wild grapes
(cultivated can be substituted and are sweeter but lack the zest)

6 ripe tomatoes
sugar according to sweetness desired
¹/₂ cup water (country well water, unchlorinated, unsoftened, for the best flavor)

Wash fruit, slice unpeeled apples and tomatoes. Remove stems and mash the grapes. Combine, add water and cook over moderate heat 15 minutes til soft...strain through cloth. Add 1 cup sugar for every 1 cup juice (depending on sweetness desired) Boil rapidly til syrup coats spoon. Pour into hot sterile jars. Seal with paraffin when cool.

CHAPTER READING SUGGESTIONS

Chapter IX . . . .Seed Catalogs and Gardening
Moshimer, Joan ***The Complete Rug Hooker - A Guide to the Craft***
(New York Graphic Society, Boston, Massachusetts 1975) A Good "How to Do" book.

Schultz, Kathlene ***Create Your Own Natural Dyes***
(Sterling Publishing Company Inc., New York 1975)

Chapter XV . . . .A Time to Dye
Kent, William Winthrop ***The Hooked Rug***
(Tudor Publishing Company, New York 1974)

Krochmal, Arnold and Konnie ***The Complete Illustrated Book of Dyes from Natural Sources***
(Double Day and Company Inc., Garden City, New York 1974)

Chapter XVII . . .Ghostly Visitors
McCutcheon, John T. ***Drawn from Memory***
(Bobbs Merrill Company Inc., Indianapolis, New York. C1950 by Evelyn Shaw McCutcheon)

Chapter XVIII . .Making Wood
Leopold, Aldo ***A Sand County Almanac***
(Oxford University Press 1949, reprint 1966)

Chapter XIX . . .Befuddled November
Breathnach, Sarah ***Mrs Sharps Traditions***
(Simon Schuster 1990)

Chapter XXIII   . .Lightning Rods and Ben Franklin
        Apps, Jerry ***Barns of Wisconsin***
        (Wisconsin Trails, Madison, Wisconsin 53705,
        revised 1995)

Chapter XXVI   . .Roads - For Whom?
        Apps, Jerry ***The Wisconsin Travelers
        Companion - A Guide to Country Sites***
        (Wisconsin Trails Inc., Madison, Wisconsin 53705
        1997)

***Wisconsin's Rustic Roads - A Road Less
Traveled***
        Five essays by: Blei, Norbert; Ferraca, Jean; Logan,
        Ben; Stokes, Bill; Vuekelich, George.
        (Lost River Press, Duluth, Minnesota 55816 1984)

***Wisconsin's Rustic Roads - A Positive Step
Backwards***
        (Free) (Wisconsin Department of Transportation, Rustic
Roads Board, P.O. Box 7913, Madison, Wisconsin
        5370-7913)

***Wisconsin's Rustic Roads - A Video Film;
Photographer Rashid, Bob.***
        (Public Broadcasting Television, 821 University
        Avenue, Madison, Wisconsin 53707)

ACKNOWLEDGMENTS

y sincere thanks to the many friends who prodded me to do this writing and supported its progress. Members of the Sheboygan County Writers' Club have earned my gratitude for listening to readings of the book's chapters and offering helpful comments and encouragement.

Writing classes at The Clearing, Ellison Bay, WI., conducted by Jerry Apps (author and Professor Emeritis, University of Wisconsin, Madison) provided the insights and perspectives I so much needed to improve my writing plus encouragement for publication. Another writing class at the clearing taught by Norbert Blei (author and small press editor/publisher) furthered my confidence about publication and gave me the push I needed to do pen and ink sketches at a time I had given up art work due to eyesight problems.

In accomplishing the pen and ink sketches I'm grateful to Joe Ash (neighbor and prize winning commercial editorial cartoonist) for his help with solving sketching problems. I also want to give credit to watercolor and sketching classes with Win Jones at The Clearing in prior years for enabling me now to undertake the sketching.

I thank my retired librarian friend, Alyce Siminow, for help with the tedious job of proof reading the manuscript. I'm also indebted to Mary Olm for the hours she so willingly and cheerfully gave in using her secretarial and computer skills in preparing final copies of my manuscript.

A very special thank you to Mike Savage and his staff who believed enough in my book to take on its publication and make this a rewarding experience.

Irene I. Luethge

ABOUT THE AUTHOR

rene I. Luethge, born in Sheboygan, WI, a descendant of the county's pioneer settlers, graduated from Sheboygan High School in 1935, attended Lawrence University, Appleton, WI received her B.A. degree in Sociology from the University of Pennsylvania, 1939, the masters of Social Work degree, 1943, then worked towards a P.h.D. degree there. She held social work and administrative positions in Philadelphia, PA, Providence, RI, Richmond, VA, New Hampshire and Cambridge, MA. She has had faculty teaching positions at Lakeland College, WI and Universities in VA, N.C., and MA., lastly at the University of Wisconsin, Madison and was also a consultant with the Wisconsin State Division of Health. Her home had become the Kettle Moraine property she writes about.

Handcrafts, her avocation interest, focussed travels in Europe and the U.S.A. on crafts people, craft guilds and folk schools. She attended classes at Rhode Island School of Design, Penland School of Handcrafts, NC, and The Clearing, Elison Bay, WI. She has won awards in art shows for her jewelry pieces and original hooked rugs dyed with plant dyes. Love of the outdoors influences her artwork.

Writing became a retirement career, spurred on by winning a couple honorable mentions in state-wide writing contests and compliments for her annual Christmas letters about country living.

Her writings have been published in: *The Journal of Social Case Work, The Doll Reader Magazine, The Milwaukee Sentinel, The Country Today, Sheboygan County Historical Society publications, New Holstein Wisconsin Reporter, The Sheboygan Press and Prime Time Magazine.* Her poetry has appeared in *The Maine Pine Cone* and the *Wisconsin Poets Calendar.*

Prize winning chapters of this book are: "Jenny", 1998, *Winner's Circle, Yarns of Yesteryear* state-wide contest. "Jenny", 1997 & "Autumn Jell", 1998 *A.P. Nelson Feature Article* state-wide contest, Wisconsin Regional Writers Association.

Other Savage Press Books:

BUSINESS
SoundBites by Kathy Kerchner
Dare to Kiss the Frog by van Hauen, Kastberg & Soden

LOCAL AND REGIONAL HISTORY, HUMOR, MEMOIR
Beyond the Mine by Peter J. Benzoni
Crocodile Tears and Lipstick Smears by Fran Gabino Jackpine
Savages, or Skinny Dipping for Fun and Profit by Frank Larson
Some Things You Never Forget by Clem Miller
Stop in the Name of the Law by Alex O'Kash
Superior Catholics by Georgeann Cheney and Teddy Meronek
Widow of the Waves by Bev Jamison

ESSAY
A Hint of Frost, Essays on the Earth by Rusty King

OUTDOORS, SPORTS & RECREATION
Cool Fishing for Kids 8 - 85 by Frankie Paull and
"Jackpine" Bob Cary
Floating All-Weather Sailboat Log Book, Coast Guard Approved
Floating Outdoor All-Weather Journals, Kayak, Canoe, Generic
The Duluth Tour Book, by Jeff Cornelius
The North Shore Tour Book by Jeff Cornelius
Stop and Smell the Cedars by Tony Jelich

POETRY
Appalachian Mettle by Paul Bennett
In the Heart of the Forest by Diana Randolph
Gleanings from the Hillsides by E. M. Johnson
Moments Beautiful - Moments Bright by Brett Bartholomaus
Pathways by Mary B. Wadzinski
Philosophical Poems by E. M. Johnson
Poems of Faith and Inspiration by E. M. Johnson
Thicker Than Water by Hazel Sangster
Treasured Thoughts by Sierra
Treasures from the Beginning of the World by Jeff Lewis

FICTION
Burn Baby Burn by Mike Savage
Keeper of the Town by Don Cameron
Something in the Water by Mike Savage
The Year of the Buffalo by Marshall J. Cook
Voices From the North Edge by St. Croix Writers

SPIRITUALITY
The Awakening of the Heart by Jill Downs
The Hillside Story by Pastor Thor Sorenson